THE
POWER
OF
PERSONAL CHANGE

Discover and Unleash the Untapped
Power Within You Through Change

CHINDAH CHINDAH

TEN THINGS THIS BOOK WILL HELP YOU LEARN AND ACHIEVE:

- 5 ways to harness the power of change in your life.
- How to maximize your potential by embracing change.
- Useful tips and advice about how to discover your personal strength assets.
- 3 proven ways to develop your strengths and use it to be more successful in life.
- The 3-pronged approach to determine the right direction that you need to go.
- Great insights into how you can cultivate consistency in your life.
- The exact process of how to take advantage of adjustments and re-evaluation.
- How to develop the qualities of an ideal behavior that breeds success.
- Discover the secret to become truly limitless in your life.
- The actual steps you need to take in order to begin pursuing your passion.

The Power of Personal Change

Copyright © 2017 by Chindah Chindah

Published by 4XL Professional Services Ltd

1ST FLOOR 2 WOODBERRY GROVE

NORTH FINCHLEY

LONDON

ENGLAND, N12 0DR

For more information about special discounts for bulk purchases,

Please email: publishing@4xlpublishing.com

Tel: 02071830366

Printed and bound in Great Britain

Legal & Disclaimer

ACKNOWLEDGEMENT

I have realized that no successful venture happens without a strong support system in place. I have been privileged to have interdependent minds and people of impeccable character and desire to ensure this book see the light of day.

Throughout the period of developing and producing this book, I felt gratitude towards the following people:

To God, my all-round mentor and coach, who inspired me first into transformational change, and motivated me to follow my purpose and passion in life.

To my beloved and supportive wife, Chimzi Chindah, who has motivated and given me the time to write this book.

To Chris and Cedric, my lovely boys, who have constantly asked me when will the book be finished.

To all my brothers and sisters, who believed in me and helped me in the way they could.

To Angie Alaya, my cover designer, who ensured the book cover was created with the right audience in mind.

To the happy memory of my father, Chief Paul Amadi Chindah.

To my mother, Mrs. Edith Chindah, for her devotion to all her nine children and for her constant demonstration of love for all.

To my mentors, Tony and Nicky Vee, for their inspiration and support in finding my purpose.

To my friends, work, and business colleagues for all their words of encouragement, especially from:

Dr. Abraham Oniku, a very good friend, who encouraged me into transformational change.

Onyinye and Ogechi Etoniru, the awesome twins, that helped and inspired me in many ways and provided suggestions and feedback.

R. T. Rulida, for your immense research contribution that went into this book

Moira Cheng, for her amazing soft personality and for believing in me to get my job done.

To all whom I am not able to list in this book, huge thanks.

CONTENTS

INTRODUCTION

"What is the limit of the human potential?" This is a question that has baffled a lot of people throughout the ages. The intricacies of human capacity, the depth of intelligence and the strength of will power have all contributed to the drastic changes that have occurred in our world. Some have used human capacity and intelligence for the betterment of our lives while others have exploited that power for selfish dreams and vain ambition. Yet, the question remains: *What will happen if a person is able to unleash that slumbering potential inside of him?*

Think about it. What if a person can have access to his inherent strengths and utilize it to improve his skill set, ergo improve his way of life? What if by changing key aspects of your mindset, attitudes, and behaviors, you can also transform the way you see the world? What if a person can unlock the secrets to living a limitless life? The possibilities of human potential are so great that a lot of other people have expressed their interest in the topic. Here are some of them:

"If we all did the things we are capable of, we would literally astound ourselves." – Thomas Edison

"The will to win, the desire to succeed, the urge to reach your full potential... These are the keys that will unlock the door to personal excellence." – Confucius

"Untapped potential is the difference between where a person is now and where he or she can be." – Bo Bennett

Do you have that same urge and desire to reach your potential? Do you have that inner voice that tells you that you are more than what you think about yourself? Do you have that nudging thought that you are capable of doing great things? Here's the clincher. I believe it's true! However, the question now is how? And that's what this book is all about.

Unleashing your potential from within

I firmly believe that every one of us has the capacity to achieve and accomplish great things if we are serious about doing so. It doesn't matter how old you are, your gender, your nationality, your profession or even your educational attainment. Every **person**, no matter who you are or what you are, has a shot at greatness. We have equal opportunities in us to harness our gift and experience success in our lives.

You might be thinking right now, how can I say that with such blunt confidence? Well, first, I am a big believer of human purpose and potential. I believe all of us have a particular calling in this life and we have the necessary tools we need to accomplish it. Secondly, I see a lot of people every day who have achieved massive success in their lives, and you know what the difference between them and those people who live beneath the surface is? Not much. Football coach and former player, Jimmy Johnson said, *"The difference between ordinary and extraordinary is that little extra."*

This book is littered with stories of famous people who achieved great things in life. You will notice that most of them also started right where you are, right now. They had nothing to boast about themselves—no fancy cars, no mansions, or millions of pesos in their bank accounts—but somehow, they were able to acquire a secret that is so important and critical that their lives were literally transformed from the inside out. The purpose of this book is to pass that 'secret' to you.

Specifically, the aim of this book is to accomplish the following objectives:

- Show you the importance of 'change' and how you can leverage on it to make your life increasingly better each day.
- Open your personal 'toolbox' and discover your unique strengths to help you improve yourself.
- Set and chart the learning pathway that will carry you faster to

2

your desired destination in life.

- Develop personal habits that aim to flesh out all the significant realizations that you have in your mind.

- Establish a robust mechanism to measure your performance and ascertain what more is required from you to do your best.

- Implement a system that will drive you towards your goal and realign you whenever your targets are off the charts, in a negative way.

- Unleashing the power of passion in your life and how you can exploit it to achieve the state of limitless living.

If these things don't excite you, then I don't know what will. This book is designed to bring out the best version of yourself by employing well-researched and time proven methods as evidenced by people who have employed these techniques. I can't overestimate the importance of learning from the example of others, so this book is filled with case studies of how people who start from the bottom end up at the pinnacle of success. It is my sincere prayer that this book will also help you in accomplishing the same feat.

Cautions and Warnings

Change has always been dangerous, especially if you are so accustomed to the way things are. A simple change in perspective and paradigm can affect a lot of people and can cause a revolution that will challenge the status quo. Change in the relationship between nations can cause wars. Change of greenhouse gasses in the atmosphere can cause drastic effects in our weather. Change in the leadership of a nation can spell disaster for a country. However, at the same time, the same change can also lead to unity, can make this world a better place and can also propel a nation to unprecedented growth. And now, that change is knocking on your door.

What will you do? Will you hold on to your old perceptions, attitudes, and mindset even if you know that it is not doing you any good? Will you continually embrace the status quo even if you realize that you can achieve greater things in your life? Will you refuse to allow change to take its course and risk living a life that is full of '*what ifs*'?

According to leadership expert John Maxwell, *"Change is inevitable, growth is optional."* Even if you don't take the challenge now, change will catch up with you eventually. So, if you don't make a change now, you won't know if it will be for good or bad?

I heard someone say that the only thing that is constant in this world is change. However, inspite of the inevitability of change, a lot of people are still afraid of it. Change increases uncertainty and forces us to go out of our comfort zones. But there is a hidden power that is available for those brave individuals who choose to embrace change in their lives. They know that they can't escape change, so instead of running away from it, they opt to welcome it with open arms and use the opportunities provided by it to improve their lives.

My goal in writing this book is to help you to honestly and sincerely be that kind of person you were intuitively designed to be. I aim to pass on to you the principles, concepts and ideas that will enable you to harness the power of change and use it to make your life better as well as the lives of people around you. It is my sincere hope that as you read the pages of this book, you will realize that change is not an enemy that we should be afraid of. Instead, I want you to realize that change can be your friend that can take you to a higher level of success and achievement in your life!

I have personally applied this principle in my life and it has dramatically changed me from the old me to a new version of myself. I know the untapped possibilities within me and I have resolved to relentlessly pursue my purpose and destiny in life with the highest level of commitment and self-discipline. The road to remarkable achievement in life has not been easy but the process of transformation has been worthwhile. You cannot discover how much you can go in life until you embrace change personally and start pushing boundaries you thought were unattainable.

You cannot escape change, so the best way to prepare for it is to proactively take hold of your future by creating it. Let this book help you in crafting a life that you truly want to live and watch your life become extraordinary!

Chindah Chindah
www.chindahchindah.com
www.limitlesslifepro.com
England, United Kingdom.

THE NEED THAT YOU DON'T SEE

CHAPTER 1

*"When we are no longer able to change a situation –
we are challenged to change ourselves."*

– Viktor Frankl

Some of us are aware of Maslow's Hierarchy of Needs. It is a simplistic yet holistic illustration of the needs of an individual from their core physiological needs like food, water and sleep to the highest need which is self-actualization. A lot of people are aware of the lower parts of the hierarchy such as our physiological needs, safety and the need to be loved and to belong. However, many of us believe that the highest aspect of the hierarchy is virtually impossible to achieve and reserved only for few selected individuals. Is this *true?*

If we measure the success of a person by his wealth, we could arrive at a staggering conclusion. In a study done by Forbes in 2016 listing the world's billionaires, they determined that the aggregate wealth of all the identified billionaires, or 0.00002% of the world's population is equal to 9% of the world's GDP. Now, it would seem that the premise is true that some things are reserved only for chosen individuals – that is if the measurement of success is wealth. However, this could not be further from the truth.

I believe success is relative and its definition will vary from one person to another. A father who was able to raise his children and give them a decent life can be considered successful. An athlete that breaks a world record can also be viewed as successful. A minister who lived in the slums of India and impacted that part of the world in a profound way can also be considered successful. The point is, success is not just about wealth. However, there is a common theme that runs through all those examples. It is the fact that those people were able to set apart themselves from the norm. And that is because they satisfy a need that you don't see.

I Still Can't See It...

If you can't still see the need that I am talking about, indulge me for a bit longer as I tell you the story of Johnetta McSwain. For more than 30 years, McSwain saw herself as inferior and a person that couldn't amount to anything. She had a detrimental view of herself, and reasons to justify that. She was born to a single mother who didn't want her and plainly told her so. Her first five or six years of her life were spent living with her grandmother in Birmingham, Alabama along with her sister and her cousin. In this place, her uncle abused them physically, sexually, emotionally and psychologically. It was a very traumatic experience for a child like her.

When her mother learned about the situation, she immediately took her children to be with her. However, the abuse did not stop. This time, the exploitation came from the men that her mother brought home. These misfortunes in her life pushed her to spend most of her time in the streets, drop out of high school and have her first child out of wedlock at the age of 19.

She had another child in her mid-twenties and without a stable job to support them, she relied on government assistance and her friends for additional support. Her sister, Sonya, summed up their situation by her statement: [Everybody in my family has been in jail, on drugs, or didn't finish high school, so what have I got to live for? What have I got to amount to? Nothing! What have I got to accomplish? Nothing.]

On her thirtieth birthday, McSwain suddenly realized she wasn't happy with her life. She wasn't satisfied with the way things were. She did not want the status quo to continue, and she knew that if she continued on her current path her two sons would also be headed for trouble. No one in her family had ever finished high school. A lot of her relatives had either died young or ended up in jail. She absolutely did not want that for her boys, so she said, *"At last, I knew it was time to make some changes."*. Her two sons finished high school eventually, and became the first set of people to make that happen in their family history.

Did you catch it? Were you able to see the need that has been hidden from your eyes for years? In case, you still don't see it, let me spell it out for you. It's C-H-A-N-G-E. Yes, I'm talking again about change. Why? Because a lot of people focus so much on their needs and wants without aiming for the one thing that could give them lasting effects – change. If you are living a life that is less than satisfactory, you need change. If you are in a situation that is detrimental to your goals and objectives in life, you need change. If you are not happy with the way things are, there is only one answer to that – change. It is the need that we usually don't see. It is a necessity in every endeavor, and successful people have a way of using it to their unfair advantage. As entrepreneur and motivational speaker, Jim Rohn, said, *"Your life does not get better by chance, it gets better by change."*

Why Do I Need It?

This book is all about change. It's all about challenging your old paradigms and perspective to show you that there might be a better life waiting on the other side. This book is founded on the principle that a highly successful life is a life that positively responds to change, be it bad or good. And in order to properly set the stage for this book, let me outline to you the five most important aspects of change in anyone's life.

1. Change allows us to evaluate our lives

There are two kinds of change that we need to face in this life. One are those events that we don't have any control over whatsoever and second, those changes that we need to proactively execute in our lives. This first point focuses on those unexpected and unavoidable changes that we encounter on a regular basis.

We have all experienced the joy of triumph and the pain of victory, we also have all felt the sadness of losing a loved one or the grief of failing in our goals. These changes can have a tremendous impact on our lives. The life of McSwain vividly illustrates this concept. Her thirtieth birthday prodded her to evaluate her life, and she did not like what she saw. However, what's amazing about her story is the simple change in her age that prompted the change and what's more amazing is she acted on it.

How about you? Whenever you experience a significant change in your life, are you also doing some evaluation and reflection to see if what you have right now matches what you actually want in your life? These events are powerful because handling it correctly has the potential to change the course of your life.

2. Change takes us out of our rut

A rut is defined in the Merriam Webster dictionary as "a long deep track made by the repeated passage of the wheels of vehicles." With regards to human behavior, a rut is "a habit or pattern of behavior that has become dull and unproductive but is hard to change." However, the most damaging aspect of a rut is its ability to go unnoticed.

We all have habits, attitudes, mindsets and perspectives that are doing us more harm than good, yet we cannot see it because we have become too accustomed to those aspects of ourselves. A particular event will happen, and those negative pieces of ourselves will be triggered like clockwork and the worst part, we don't even know that it is in there. We see it as perfectly reasonable.

Look at the story of McSwain. For 30 years, with all the negative experiences that she had, she settled in a rut that shouted of her incapability, lack of knowledge, and that she did not deserve anything good in her life. The real condition of her life and the direction that she was orchestrating for her sons, was hidden behind the ruts that had been developed decades ago. However, an honest assessment in the mirror broke it. Her change in age – her birthday – was followed by a shift in mindset and that took her out of her rut.

What are the ruts that are continually shaping you and worsening the condition of your life? For me, a simple way of identifying a rut is to evaluate my life experiences. What are those events and circumstances that always bring out the worst in you? Perhaps there is a particular perspective, paradigm, and mindset – a rut – that has caused this. Embrace change and eventually, you will be able to get rid of those harmful ruts. As author, Mandy Hale, said, "Growth is painful, change is painful, but nothing is as painful as staying stuck somewhere you don't belong."

3. Change helps you to achieve your goals

I will share some interesting trivia with you. Do you know that all flights, whether short or long distance, are off-course 99% of the time? So how are these aircraft able to land at the right destination?

Simple. Because throughout the whole time that they are in the air, aircraft are consistently making course corrections. In short, they utilize change in order to achieve their goals.

The same can be said of the principle of accomplishment. We cannot achieve what we want to achieve if we are not willing to implement changes every now and then. In fact, just staying on the right course will not guarantee that you will arrive at your desired destination. Stage actor, Will Rogers, said, *"Even if you're on the right track, you'll get run over if you just sit there."* Accomplishments are for those people who constantly move and who continuously embrace change.

No matter how great your potential is, it won't matter if you are not willing to make some changes in yourself. Think about this: What if a person has the potential to be a great doctor? However, instead of studying, all he does is watch TV, surf the internet and go to parties. Do you think he will be able to achieve his goal and unleash his potential to become a doctor? Absolutely not! Without change, potential is useless. Without change, goals will be unreachable.

The story of Thomas Edison is one of the greatest illustrations of the importance of change in achieving your goals. Edison's greatest accomplishment is perhaps the incandescent light bulb. However, this feat was not accomplished that easily. In fact, Edison's quote about the process that he underwent in the invention of this light bulb is so famous and is continually used in a lot of books and motivational talks.

Edison said, "*I have not failed. I've just found 10,000 ways that won't work.*" Though 10,000 might be considered an exaggeration, the core idea of what he said remains intact: change combined with unyielding determination made possible the accomplishment of Thomas Edison's goals.

4. Change impacts the people around you

Have you watched the movie, *Groundhog Day*? It's a fantastic comedic film which tells the story of meteorologist, Phil Connors, and how he mysteriously lived the *Groundhog Day* over and over again every day. Its concept is hilarious. However, the ideas that the movie presented are truly thought-provoking. What will you do if you are to live the same day repeatedly? Will you also repeat the routine or will you live each day to improve yourself from yesterday?

For Connors, the idea of change was simple; since he was living on a loop he took advantage of it to win the heart of the girl he loved. Every mistake that he made, he avoided it the next day and eventually, he got the girl. However, at the same time, the loop also helped him to evaluate his life – his priorities, his goals and his ambitions. And upon realizing the need to change, he changed himself and impacted all the people around him. People began to say, *"What happened to you? Tell us. We want that too!"*

Change is not for individual consumption only. Whenever there is change, expect that it will also create a ripple effect on the people who surround you. Again, the case of McSwain is a great illustration of this concept. Her decision to change herself from a loser single-mother to a successful individual affected not only her but also the lives of her sons and even the people that she got to know. That is because change is always contagious.

Think about this: why do we get inspired whenever we hear a story of a person who overcomes an addiction? Or an individual who started from the slums and eventually worked his way to the top? Or a person who created a significant impact in his community? Because, deep inside of us, we all desire change. We want to experience its power and its ability to improve our lives. Change is infectious, and once you have experienced it, you can't stop sharing it with other people. When you undergo the change process, it also gives you the power to inspire others to act and do their part in improving their lives.

5. *Change gives us a shot to level up our lives*

Basketball legend John Wooden said, *"Things turn out best for people who make the best of the way things turn out."* If there is one thing that is eternally constant in this world it is change. We cannot escape it, and we cannot run away from it. No matter how old you are, regardless of your gender and even your disposition in life, you will always experience change. However, though we cannot escape it, we can always choose our response to it. The choice has always been in our hands.

Change is like a wave. It can either crush us or bring us to greater heights. If you are looking for opportunities to level up your life, then there's no other way but to embrace change and to take on the challenge of improving yourself. In fact, most of the time, during those painful changes, we are forced to change ourselves to cope.

"Every painful experience has an embedded message for you to leverage to your advantage and advancement, as you transform to a new version of yourself" – Chindah Chindah

One day, a frog was hopping down the road when he fell down a large and deep pothole. The frog tried its best to climb out of the hole, but all his best efforts were in vain. A rabbit saw him and tried to help – to no avail. More animals came from the forest to rescue the frog, however they were not still able to remove him from the deep pit. In exhaustion, the rabbit said, *"Well, looks like you will stay there a little longer. Friends, let us get some food to regain our strength and perhaps we can think of another way to rescue this poor fellow."* So they left him and walked away.

After a few seconds, to their surprise they heard the frog hopping out towards them! One of the animals said, "Wow! How did you do that? A minute before, we could do nothing to rescue you, but now, here you are! How did you climb out of that pothole?" "Well," answered the frog, "I really can't climb. But I

12

heard a truck coming my way, and I knew I needed to jump out!"

Times, we are tested or in the midst of great struggles and problems, are also able to bring out the best in you, to change your life for the better, and to experience a breakthrough. Writer Joseph Campbell said, "Opportunities to find deeper powers within ourselves come when life seems most challenging."

The Need for Change

Humans are designed for change. The mere fact that our physical bodies, the way we think, and even our perspective in life are continually changing is a testament that we are creatures of change. The only question is how we are using its power to impact our lives for the better.

At the beginning of this chapter, I told you the story of Johnetta McSwain and her struggles in life. Upon recognizing the need to change when she turned 30 years old, she immediately did her part in sorting out her life. With no support from her family, she decided to pursue college by leaving everything in her hometown of Birmingham.

After three years of trying hard to move out and go to Atlanta, Georgia, she was able to pull it off. She enrolled at Kennesaw State University and challenged herself by taking more than a full load every semester. However, since she had stopped study for almost a decade, she struggled a lot when it came to academics. That did not stop her. Her determination to experience change and to improve her life for herself and her sons was stronger than the hardships she encountered.

Johnetta said, "I realized I didn't have to be smart. I just had to be determined, motivated and focused. This came with a high price tag for me. I had to change my thinking. I had to think like a smart person." And that she did. In order to help herself in changing the way she thought, she sought out the most intelligent person in each of her classes and she studied with them. Soon enough, she was studying and achieving academic excellence as the best student in her school. And within three years, she was able to finish her bachelor's degree. After seven more years, she had completed her doctorate degree.

Johnetta's story is an excellent example of a person who saw the need for change and embraced it. She used the hurtful experiences in the past, the scarred self-image that she had and the painful realizations about her life as stepping stones to change. And the best thing with the change is that as she underwent it, it also impacted the lives of people around her.

What is your story? Are you undergoing a painful struggle right now that you just want to escape? Or perhaps you feel frustrated about yourself? Do you want to do great things, help other people, and want your life to matter, but somehow, you cannot muster the strength that you need to start? As someone wisely commented, "Most people are comfortable with old problems than with new solutions." I hope that won't be the case for you.

"The only way to overcome some problems in life is to go through the problems and maximize the opportunities the problems will bring, to make you seek and create a solution" – Chindah Chindah.

This book is an advocate of change. If you have been challenged by this initial chapter, expect that you will be challenged all throughout this book to discover deeper aspects of yourself and at the same time implement any improvement that you need so you can become the best version of yourself. It is my sincere hope that as you continually read the pages of this manuscript, you will also be enlightened about the different areas of your life that need to be changed. And that will be the subject of the next chapter.

Discussion Questions and Reflections:

This portion of each chapter aims to establish the concepts and principles that you have learned so far. Try to carefully consider each question and answer it with a complete reflection of how it applies to your life. I would also implore you to take notes and even share what you have learned with others to initiate healthy discussion.

1. Do you believe that all people need change in their life? Based on your own assessment of your life, how can you say that change is urgently needed to happen? Can you identify a particular scenario where you are forced to change any aspect of yourself, such as your attitude, your way of talking, or even the way you see things compared to others?

2. Have you experienced significant change recently or even in the past? Looking back at what happened, what is the greatest lesson that you have learned about change? In the five specific reasons that I outlined in this chapter, what do you think is the benefit you have received pertaining to the change that you mentioned? Here is the summary of the "Five Important Aspects of Change" to help you in answering these questions:

    *   Change allows us to evaluate our lives.
    *   Change takes us out of our rut.
    *   Change helps you to achieve your goals.
    *   Change impacts the people around you.
    *   Change gives us a shot to level up our lives.

3. What is the lesson you gleaned from the story of Johnetta McSwain? Is there any similarity between yours and her life story? How can you use your past pains and struggles to challenge yourself to achieve greater things in your life? How can you create an impact in the lives of the people around you?

_____

_____

_____

THE GEAR THAT WILL
TAKE YOU THERE!

CHAPTER 2

*"You cannot change your destination overnight, but you
can change your direction overnight."*

— *Jim Rohn*

What is the fastest way to get from point A to point B? Normally, it will depend on the road that you take. A straight road will probably get you faster to your desired destination, while a long and winding road will possibly take you a longer time. The mechanism that you use will also affect your arrival time. Using a high-speed Ferrari will give you a shorter travel time compared to using a single gear Japanese bicycle. The speed at which you arrived at the place you want to go is directly related to the road and the means of travel that you used to get there. The same is true with change.

A lot of people aim to accomplish something — to arrive at *"Destination Success"* — without properly considering the road they are taking and the vehicle they are using. Change will not result in significant advancement if you err in choosing your direction for change and the means you will use to achieve it. For instance, if you are in the city of London and using a map of Birmingham, then you are highly guaranteed to fail in reaching your desired destination. Also, using a pogo stick to travel on the busy roads of the city will definitely increase your time of travel.

"To succeed at anything, you must know exactly what your target is; don't meander around directionless. Directionless people are not focused people" — Chindah Chindah.

In Chapter 1, I introduced to you the concept of change and its role in accomplishing great things in your life. Change is also instrumental in overcoming any undesired state and stepping up to a new level in your way of living. We have established the need for change and at the same time outlined the specific benefits that an individual will obtain once he embraces it in his daily life. In this chapter, we will go deeper into the topic of change by identifying the essential elements of change and particularly establishing and determining the direction of change that a person must take in order to arrive at "*Destination Success.*"

Change and Its Basic Elements

Writer and leadership speaker, Robin Sharma, once said, *"Change is hard at first, messy in the middle and gorgeous at the end."* I firmly believe that one of the foundations of being human is having the capacity to respond to change. Since we cannot escape the realities of it, we are usually forced to embrace it or to make our lives miserable by resisting it. To properly weather the drastic effects of change in your life, you need to have a proper understanding of the essential elements that compose it.

1. The Need for Change

We have established the need for change in Chapter 1. As individuals who aspire for great achievements, change can be your best friend or your worst enemy. A sound understanding of our need to change will give us a better perspective in coping with its effects in our lives. If there is no change, there is no growth, and if there is no growth, there are no accomplishments. As J P Morgan said, *"The first step towards getting somewhere is to decide that you are not going to stay where you are."* In short, embrace the need for change.

2. The Desire for Change

Knowing the need for change is not enough if you still don't have the desire for it. A person who acts like this becomes so frustrated with his life because he knows that he needs to change something yet he lacks the power to act on it. If you are a student

18

and getting low grades because of your weak efforts in your studies, then the knowledge that you need change comes naturally.

However, having the knowledge is not enough. If you don't desire to overcome your struggles in class, if you don't wish to get a good grade and you don't want to shape up when it comes to your academic performance, then guess what will happen to the need for change? It will be frustrated, along with the possible achievements that you get.

3. The Capacity for Change

Alright, now that you have cultivated the desire for change. It is a significant step towards experiencing its profound effect on your life. Now, the next step would be to act on it. You do this by developing your capacity for change. Three particular areas of our lives – mind, words, and actions – will propel us towards the benefits of change or will hinder us in achieving it.

You might not be aware of it, but you are in a constant molding process through these three things. For instance, if you are an employee and you sincerely desire to be promoted in your job, then you know you need to exceed expectations. If you are performing at a low level, then change is necessary to make your promotion possible. However, if your mind is full of negativity, your mouth will always utter bad things, and you don't change your actions towards your work, then promotion will be out of reach.

4. The Direction of Change

The last element of change is having the right direction towards where you need to go. What are the things that you need to turn away from? Is there a need to change your course towards success? Do you need to shift your gears to reflect more of your priorities? These are important questions that need to be answered when it comes to establishing and determining the direction of change you need to go through.

The remainder of this chapter will focus on elaborating these core elements of change. I encourage you to carefully reflect everything you are about to read since this chapter is instrumental to the successful implementation of the techniques and advice outlined in the successive chapters of this book.

Cultivating Your Desire for Change

It is one thing to determine that you need to change, it is another thing to desire sincerely that change to happen. Let's face it: every day of our lives, we are confronted with the brutal fact that our lives need major overhauling. However, due to our own predisposition to stay in our comfort zone, few of us rarely cultivate the necessary desire for change.

The life of Jim Rohn is a great illustration of someone who saw the need for change and at the same time developed his inner desire to live a better life. Jim Rohn grew up on a farm in Idaho. He graduated from high school, however, after going to college for one year, he decided to call it quits. He said, *"One year of college and I thought I was thoroughly educated."*

After leaving his life as a college student, he went on to work as a stock clerk at Sears, but like the situation of typical employees, Rohn lived from paycheck to paycheck. It's not the life that he wished for and by age 25, he became truly discouraged. Fortunately for him and the rest of the world, Jim Rohn did not stop there. He used the frustrations and struggles of his current life to cultivate his desire to change.

One day a friend invited him to attend a seminar by motivational speaker and salesman, J. Earl Shoaff. The central message of the workshop was this: *Work harder on yourself than you do on your job; your earnings are directly related to your philosophy, not the economy, and for things to change, you must change.* The message struck at his heart like lightning and further fueled his desire for change.

If you are currently in the process of cultivating your desire for change, let these three things help you in enforcing that idea in your mind as you pursue the idea of change:

1. The Desire to Overcome

Why do most people fail in effecting change in their lives? Is it because of the overwhelmingly huge tasks that are set before them? Or is it because of the complexity of the process that they need to go through? Or perhaps it's because of the enormous problem that they need to face? Well, all these things might contribute to the failure of change. However, I believe the greatest reason why we fail to implement transformation is because of deeply rooted complacency. Comfort has always been the enemy of achievement. We don't want to change because we are too comfortable sitting on the cushion of our long-time situation.

To cultivate the desire for change, we must grow and nurture our desire to overcome. We must continually remind ourselves we are created for something bigger, that there is more to life than what we are living right now. Jim Rohn recognized this. He realized that there was more to life than living from paycheck to paycheck. In one of his famous sayings, he said, *"Don't wish it were easier; wish you were better. Don't wish for less problems; wish for more skills. Don't wish for less challenges; wish for more wisdom."* Life is all about overcoming yourself, your circumstances and your inner desire for complacency.

2. The Desire for New Life

Another component of cultivating the desire for change is aspiring to have a new life. It's all about having a perspective that recognizes that there are greater things waiting for us on the other side of change. What are the things that you don't really need, but you still hold on to? Are those things hindering you from becoming the person you were created to be? If you are not happy with what you are receiving from life, then it's time to implement some major overhaul in the way you do things.

A father took two sisters of about the same age to the public swimming pool. Lucy, the elder one, acquired a deep passion for swimming. Every day she asked her father to take her to the public pool so she could practice and hone her skills to prepare for competitions. And boy, she practiced hard! However, Mary, the younger one, did not share the same passion. She was content to watch TV and eat her favorite chocolate chip cookies.

Lucy's love for the sport and her desire to win medals fueled her passion for continuous practice. She was relentless in pursuing her dreams and eventually, her efforts paid off. She won medals and trophies from different competitions and eventually participated in contests outside her hometown. One day, her younger sister, Mary was walking towards the kitchen and caught a glimpse of the numerous medals hanging on the living room wall. She asked her father who was watching TV, *"Daddy, why don't I have any medals?"*

Most people are like Mary. They want the medals and trophies of success, but they are not willing to do the hard work necessary to achieve it. To increase your desire for change, you must also amplify your desire for new life. It means that you must also be willing to do whatever is necessary to achieve the goals you have set for yourself.

3. The Desire to Have a Lasting Impact

This third point is for those people who have already transitioned to successful living. Impact comes from sharing what you have with other individuals with the aim of making their lives significantly better. Unfortunately, you cannot give what you don't have. Before you can desire for lasting impact, your life must experience some kind of impact first.

Now if you are that person who already has some success under your belt, then this desire must also propel your passion for undergoing more change in your life. The goal of every individual must be to leave this world a little better than they have found it. Cultivating a desire for lasting impact will help you to transition from living for yourself to living to help other people.

Unleashing the Capacity for Change

John Porter said, *"People underestimate their capacity for change. There is never a right time to do a difficult thing."* Change is always difficult, it always connotes struggle and resistance and rightly so, because we are wired with a tendency to be too comfortable with our situation.

In fact, most people will choose to stay where they are, even if it is not in their best interests, just to avoid the pain of undergoing change. However, if you have already decided you need to implement some changes in your life, then start with these three specific areas.

1. Change Your Mind-set

Everything starts with the mind. Whatever you think in your mind will find its way out through your words or the way that you act. Successfully navigating the process of change includes changing your mindset as a prerequisite. That is because you cannot change your life without changing the way you think. Norman Vincent Peale, the author of the bestseller, *The Power of Positive Thinking,* said, *"Change your thoughts and change your world."* His book is a testament to the power of a person's mind in implementing change in his life.

In a particular story that showed what a difference a changed mind can make, Dr. Peale shared an account of how a limo driver was able to change his perspective by filling his mind with positive thoughts. One winter morning, the driver fetched Dr. Peale and drove him to a lecture engagement in another town about 35 miles away. Since it was winter, the road was kind of slippery, but the driver was going a little fast which made Dr. Peale kind of nervous. He reminded the driver that they had plenty of time, so they could take it easy.

During the course of their conversation, the driver explained that he had been negative most of time and had lived with a defeated mindset. His pessimistic tendency not only affected him, but the lives of people around him, his performance at work and his life in general. In his words, the driver had lived a *"miserable life."* However, all these negativities banished upon employing a simple technique of personal change

The driver kept on hand a pack of small cards where positive affirmations was written. All he did was read these words repeatedly, and in time, he was able to change his mind from one that is utterly pessimistic, to one that was wonderfully positive. And by changing his mindset, everything changed for him – from his personal life to his relationships and even in his business.

If you are contemplating a change that will drastically affect your mindset, then take this advice from Dr. Peale himself:

"Feelings of confidence depend upon the type of thoughts that habitually occupy your mind. Think defeat and you are bound to feel defeated. But practice thinking confident thoughts, make it a dominating habit, and you will develop such a strong sense of capacity that regardless of what difficulties arise you will be able to overcome them."

2. Change your Words

Do you know you are continuously talking to yourself all throughout the day? It might not be an audible conversation, but you are always communicating with yourself through different inner monolog sessions. Psychologists identified one important category of these inner conversations as *"self-talk."* This self-talk pertains to the process in which you provide opinions and assessments on what you are doing as you are doing it. Self-talk is critical to your success because it will either reinforce your thrust towards success or will hinder your move to achieve your goals.

Athletes are known to practice this self-talk when competing with others. In fact, they do it audibly in the hearing of others. If you've heard of this idea before, you may have thought athletes were out of their mind. In one instance, tennis star Tommy Haas was captured on video doing his self-talk while taking a break from an intense match. It was part of his mental game and had been instrumental in helping him win matches. Written below is the transcription of his self-talk in that match.

"You can't win that way, Haas. It's not possible. It doesn't work that way. It doesn't work. Just too weak. Too many errors. Too many errors. It is always the same.

I don't want this anymore. I don't feel like it. Why am I doing all this *expletive*? For what? For whom? Except for myself. Why? For which reason? I can't do it. I don't get it. I'm paying people for nothing. For absolutely nothing. That I can get excited over it. You're a retard.

24

Once again, you didn't go to the net. Nicely done. But you're gonna win.

You'll win that match, come on! You can't lose it. Fight!"

It has long been debated by coaches and psychologists alike whether self-talk can affect the performance of athletes. And multiple studies have identified the relationship between these inner monologs and the function of a person. Try it out for yourself. For the coming days, control your thoughts and talk positively about yourself. Affirm your strengths, and appreciate your uniqueness. Encourage yourself that you can do what you are setting yourself to do.

"What you say with your mouth, you impress in your heart" – Dr. W. F. Kumuyi

If you are not yet convinced of the great power that changing your words can do in your life, then consider this example. Two employees were given the exact same task not to cooperate but to achieve their best within a specified amount of time. The first employee was deeply frightened of the challenge that was put in front of him. He said to himself:

"I can't do this. I am not prepared for this kind of task. What if I fail? What if I ruin this? I might lose my job! Oh, my! How will I provide for my family? I can't do this. It's too hard. I'm done for."

The second employee was equally challenged with the task, but unlike the first employee, this is what he said to himself:

"I can do this. I have prepared myself to tackle this kind of task. It's hard, but what if I succeed? What if I finish this exceptionally well? I might be promoted! Oh my! I can provide more for my family! I can do this! Nothing is too hard for me! This is my time!"

Who do you think will finish the task according to what the employer wants? Who do you think will be successful in the long run? Looking at the way these two employees conducted their self-talk, you can easily get an idea of how these two people will perform their tasks. If you are to engage your capacity for change, then you need to change your words, especially the way you talk to yourself.

Don't let any negative self-talk drag you down to a level where your belief in yourself is so low you can't even start thinking about the possibilities of change in your life.

3. Change your Actions

Your thinking and your words will not amount to anything if you fail to implement the essential actions needed to change your life. In the field of architecture and engineering, a meticulous blueprint will just be reduced to ink and paper if the people fail to build the actual structure. It's the same with our lives. Good intentions demand actions. That is where true and lasting transformation lies. However, in addition to acting out your plans, it also vital that you perform the right actions. For instance, if you are planning to build a 100-storey structure, then you can't excavate a foundation for a 20-storey building only. Your actions must match the intensity of your plans.

To improve your chances of getting your actions right, then consider the following guidelines:

a. Start Small

Apple co-founder, Steve Jobs, said, "Start small, think big. Don't worry about too many things at once. Take a handful of simple things to begin with, and then progress to more complex ones." A lot of people fail to act because they are overwhelmed by the enormity of the task ahead of them. They try to overcome all the obstacles before they even begin; therefore, they never actually begin.

By starting small and committing yourself consistently to take small steps towards success, you also build your confidence to try riskier endeavors in the future. Remember, the boy David defeated the giant Goliath using only a small pebble. You too can slay the enormous tasks ahead by focusing on small actions one step at a time.

b. Be Consistent

If there is one challenging aspect of taking actions towards change, it is the challenge of consistency. We are all guilty of this. We set goals for ourselves and do it without fail in the beginning. However, as time goes by, the initial motivation and excitement will wane as well as our actions. "Every day" will change to "most days" then turn to "some days" until we find ourselves not doing it at all.

To help ourselves be consistent, we need to find the discipline to schedule our actions. Make it a routine. Hang a written goal on your wall so you can visualize the *"finish line"* you want to reach. If possible, find a person that will remind you of your commitment and will keep you accountable in your actions.

c. Finish Strong

If you are to be successful in this area of your life, then you need to finish what you began. And I must admit this is the hardest part of change. In fact, according to a study conducted by Statistic Brain Research Institute, out of all the people who make New Year's Resolution, only a miniscule 9.2% feel they are successful in achieving what they have set at the end of the year.

It is encouraging to see a person who starts to do something for the first time. It speaks of his courage, boldness, and belief in what he wants to achieve. However, as I grow older, I have realized what is truly encouraging is to see someone who has the fortitude to finish what he began. Many people start, but only a few finishes. The question now is: *Where do you stand in regards to what you planned to do a while ago?*

The Direction of Change

A couple was driving down the freeway when they noticed their navigation app was telling them to take a right turn on a nearby street. The driver knew the road was not yet paved and therefore would give them a hard time driving. However, at the same time, they wondered why the app had told them to turn right. Because they didn't want to be bothered by the inconvenience of a bumpy ride and the possibility of traveling longer, they opted to disregard the suggestion.

About five miles into the ride, the couple had to stop because all the vehicles ahead of them were not moving. The guy opened his window and stuck out his head to see the reason for the traffic jam, and saw a large, 20-wheeler tanker lying on its side in the center of the freeway. Before they can move back, other vehicles pulled in behind them. Now, they were stuck, and they waited for five hours before the huge tanker was removed.

Most of us are like the couple in the story. We don't want to deviate from what we already know. Perhaps, it is because of our foreknowledge that the road to change will be bumpy and uncomfortable. Or maybe because we believe that the current road we are taking will get us to our destination faster. Little do we know that the path we are travelling leads to a dead end, and when we reach that point of no turning back, we are reduced to telling ourselves, "*If only I changed my direction back there.*"

Change doesn't come easy. If it did, then a lot of people would be doing it every single day. I will be bold to say that positive change is reserved only for those individuals who are worthy enough to pursue it. It doesn't matter how old you are, what you do in life, or what your past experiences are. If you want to be successful and unleash that potential inside of you, then you need to embrace change and work hard to achieve it.

"The quality of your life will be measured and determined by the clarity of your vision and the authenticity of your change of direction in life" – Chindah Chindah.

The great philosopher, Socrates, once said, *"The secret of change is to focus all of your energy, not on fighting the old, but on building the new."* You are able, you have the capacity, and most importantly, you have the choice to implement change in every aspect of your life. It is needed. It is vital. There is no other way because it is the "gear" that will take you to different places.

28

Discussion Questions and Reflections:

This portion of each chapter aims to establish the concepts and principles that you have learned so far. Try to carefully consider each question and answer it with a complete reflection of how it applies to your life. I would also implore you to take notes and even share what you have learned with others to initiate healthy discussion.

1. In this chapter, we have covered the topics that further implore you to implement change in your life. Of the four elements of change, namely, the need, the desire, the capacity, and the direction of change, what excites you most and why? List some of the prevailing aspects of your life that you want to change and answer the following:

   a. Why do you need that change?

   b. Do you desire to have that change? Why or why not?

   c. What capacity do you have to effect that change?

   d. What is the direction that you need to experience change in that aspect?

   _____

   _____

   _____

2. There are a lot of motivations and reasons why we desire change in our lives. Some reasons are stronger and much more compelling compared to others, for instance life and death situations, or when the future of a loved one is at stake. It is essential that you can properly identify the sources of those desires. In relation to your answer to the first question, list your reasons and motives for experiencing change. Write down three to five reasons and rank them based on their strength and impact on your life.

   _____

   _____

3. We all have the capacity to improve our lives and to improve the lives of people around us. However, for most people, these capacities are lying dormant and therefore cannot cause the positive changes that they want to experience. In this chapter, I outlined to you the three different ways to unleash that capacity. So, in relation to your answers to the question above, write down your specific action plan *(change in mindsets)*, declarations, *(change in words)*, and activities to perform *(change in actions)* that can help you see change in the way you live your life.

_____

_____

_____

OPENING YOUR TOOLBOX

CHAPTER 3

"The same boiling water that softens the potato hardens the egg. It's about what you're made of, not the circumstances."

– Anonymous

Self-improvement and personal development is at the heart of a successful life. Ask the student who graduated Suma Cum Laude and he will tell you that his success in academics is due to unrelenting efforts studying and learning everything he needed to get a high grade. Ask an Olympic gold medalist and she will tell you that countless hours of training and practice with the right mix of determination was the key to her success. Ask the billionaire businessman and he will tell you that his success was not achieved overnight but through continuous development and adaptation to the growing complexity of his trade.

"Your overall significance in life is directly linked to your continuous development of yourself" – Chindah Chindah.

If you are serious in changing your life for the better, then you must embrace the idea of self-improvement. Jim Rohn wisely commented, *"Work hard at your job and you can make a living. Work hard on yourself and you can make a fortune."* The idea of success is achievable as long as you play by its rules. And one important rule that you must never forget is this: *Develop and improve yourself to unleash your highest potential.*

Look around you. Examine the lives of successful people. Evaluate their experiences, principles, and beliefs. You will see that these people put a high premium on personal growth. They know their chances of accomplishing great things are being improved or diminished only by themselves. So, they work hard on what they know. They read books to learn more about their craft. They talk to great people that can give them ideas. And they attend events and seminars to hone whatever skills they have.

However, any serious endeavor to grow yourself starts with knowing and appraising yourself first. You need to know who you are and what you can bring to the table before you actually bring yourself to the table. Writer, Virginia Woolf, quipped, *"Without self-awareness we are as babies in the cradles."* In short, without knowing ourselves, and our strengths, we will remain powerless to the circumstances around us. Therefore, it is crucial to be aware of who you really are and one aspect that demands important attention is determining your personal strengths.

From Failure to Success

There is a story that illustrates the importance of knowing your strengths and capitalizing on it. John James Audubon, a son of a French sea captain, was born in Haiti in 1785. He spent his childhood in France and was educated to become a gentleman, yet because of his poor performance and attitude towards his class, he was sent to military school at the age of 14. However, his performance in the military school didn't improve because his real passion was hunting and drawing birds.

Upon reaching adulthood, Audubon tried his luck in business. His first venture involved dealing in indigo dye which lost him a small fortune. After that, he worked at the import business, but as with his first venture he had no success. But Audubon's tenacity was unwavering. Next, he tried retail trade and through his father's connections, he was able to start another business with his partner, Ferdinand Rozier, a young French businessman. They moved to Louisville, Kentucky and set up their establishment, which met with minimal success.

After working together for a while, their business struggled financially and was in deep financial trouble. Without enough money of his own, Audubon sold his wife's share of her family estate to pay off their creditors. Upon settling their debts, the partners decided to move to Henderson, Kentucky to continue their trade, thinking that a new location is what they needed. After six months, they moved again to the banks of Mississippi, but still they encountered some difficulties there. Finally, they set up their store in Ste. Genevieve, Missouri. However, it seemed success still evaded them. So, in time, Audubon sold his share to his partner and they went their separate ways.

Though he had always worked in the field of commerce, Audubon's passion for hunting, drawing and painting birds did not diminish. His biographer, John Chancellor said, *"Audubon believed that he should persevere in commerce and that shooting, mounting, and drawing birds should remain an absorbing hobby."* Yes, the man had the tenacity and persevering spirit to continue in spite of his failures, but it seemed that these things are not enough to give him the success that he desperately wanted.

Looking at his life right now, one could say that maybe he was not just in the right place at the right time. However, his life told a different story. For most of his life, Audubon pursued success outside his personal strengths. How can I say that? Because Audubon became successful, not in commerce, but in the area, he truly loved and where his true competency lay – painting birds.

Defining Strength

Audubon's story is one of those unique accounts of failing in an area of life in spite of great effort and hard work, only to know that he was molded for something entirely different. It also speaks of the importance of identifying and determining your strengths if you truly want to become successful in this life. But before we go into that aspect of ascertaining your personal strengths, let us have a clear definition first of what is strength.

For most people, the word strength conjures up images of super heroes like Superman, the Hulk or the X-Men. These fictional characters define how strength is commonly viewed, which is typically defined by super human abilities, powers, and extraordinary intellect. Some people see strength only in the context of physical capability. They think of heavy lifters, guys with huge biceps and muscle-toned bodies, and athletes who compete. Is this the real definition of strength? If it is, then people who have physical handicaps or thin bodies will always be considered weak. No, the concept of strength has a deeper and more profound meaning and cannot be equated with muscular abilities.

To provide a more comprehensive idea of what strength truly is, here are some different definitions about strength:

"Strength is the ability to consistently provide near-perfect performance in a specific activity." – Gallup

"Strength is an ability. To be strong is to have ability. In life, in the gym, and in relationships. The ability to overcome the physical, emotional, or subjective obstacles that hinder our progress as human beings. That is strength." – Better Movement

"Strength is the foundation for all of an athlete's performance traits." – Power Athlete

Based on these definitions we can come up with our own definition of strength in the context of personal life. For the purposes of this chapter, and this book *"Strength is a person's ability – whether gifted or acquired – that he can use to improve his overall performance in any aspect of life."* If you want to be successful, then you need to identify and work hard on improving your strengths. That's what this chapter is all about.

Truths about Strength

To further understand the principles and concepts of strength and to provide a deeper foundation about its ideas, we also need to get a good grasp of the different truths about our strengths. Though, there are a lot of definitions, there are some basic qualities of strength, be they physical, emotional or intellectual.

1. Strength is common and different at the same time

Strength is a common ability for every individual. We all have strengths that lie within us that are waiting to be used to improve our lives. The student in the elementary grade, the quarterback playing in the field, the single mother who is raising her children and the war veteran who is spending his remaining days in the home for the aged – all these people have strengths.

However, the category, the level, and the development of strengths vary from individual to individual. It is what makes strengths different for each person. We may both have strength in academics, but we can clearly say that your intelligence is different to mine and vice versa. Just because someone does not excel in mathematics class doesn't means that he is weak entirely. It may be possible that his area of strengths lies in a different subject.

2. Strength is Embryonic

Our strengths have the capability to grow and to improve. If you can lift a 30lb dumbbell today, then surely you can lift a 50lb dumbbell in the near future. If you can handle the pressure of working for five hours straight on your project, then there is a high probability that you can handle working for eight hours as well.

With proper training and practice, our strengths can grow and develop until they reach their maximum potential. Guaranteed, this process may not be comfortable, but remember, there is always a resistance on that path of change.

It also doesn't change the fact that if you could choose to improve what you do now, you probably would. Let what James E. Faust, religious leader, lawyer and politician said, encourage you: *"If you take each challenge one step at a time, with faith in every footstep, your strength and understanding will increase."*

3. Strength is Complimentary

Your strength complements your passion. Whatever intrinsic desire you must achieve lies within you, the inherent strengths you have will also help you to accomplish them. The story of the lost eagle illustrates this point powerfully.

One day, the mother eagle dropped her egg in a nearby farm. It was a good thing that the location where it fell was a barn with lots of hay and straw, so the egg was unharmed. The farmer saw the egg and thought it must be a hen's egg so he immediately put it in the hen's nest along with the other chicken eggs. Then, time came for the eggs to be hatched. Of course, the baby eagle saw nothing wrong with anything except he was slightly different in appearance from the other chicks. Well, who cared? For all he knew, he was a chicken!

So, the baby eagle grew up with the chicks. And since he believed that the hen was his mother, so he lived the life of a chicken. He walked like a chicken, ate like a chicken, and chirped like a chicken. However, every day a large eagle would fly above them and deep in the heart of this young eagle, he also desired to fly. But he couldn't do it. For all he knew, he was a chicken.

The young eagle grew to be an adult and all this time, he had this burning desire in his heart to fly and then an idea struck him, *"What if I try?"* So, he walked towards a nearby cliff, his heart beating fast, while saying to himself, *"All my life, I have wanted to fly. However, for all I know, I'm just a chicken. But if I die today, then so be it. At least I will be named the most courageous chicken of all time."* And with that, he jumped, opened his wings, and he flew towards the horizon.

What's the moral of the story? People are always passionate about something. For some it is evid while in others some digging is required before they discover it. Whatever it is for you, it is important to remember that your strengths complement your passion. Learning what you love doing the most is one way to determine the specific strengths that you have.

Categories of Strengths

Strength is a broad term that encompasses the whole aspect of human life. In fact, you might not be aware that you are using personal strength assets all throughout the day to accomplish things you need to finish and work on towards the goal you want to achieve. In order to properly identify the personal strengths, you have, we need to have an understanding first of the different categories of strengths. This list is not conclusive and deeper analysis and assessment can further subdivide these categories, but for now, here are the major ones.

1. Intellectual Strength

This is the capacity of an individual to think, analyze, imagine and solve problems using the strength of his mind. People with intellectual strength show an advanced understanding of the way things are. They are not limited to the facts that are presented to them; rather they have the ability to properly evaluate the conclusiveness of evidence presented and assess its relevance in solving a specific problem.

Intellectual strength is normally measured using the Intelligent Quotient (I.Q.) and based on these parameters we can note some people who have tremendous intellectual strength: Terrence Tao with a verified IQ of 230, Christopher Hirata with 225, and Kim Ung-Yong who has a verified IQ of 210.

However, to say that the intellectual strength of a person can only be measured using their IQ would be misleading. Yet, that aspect of the human mind will be further elaborated through other sources. Suffice to say that intellectual strength will help you to reinvent yourself, solve different issues in your life, and get you to a higher level of living.

2. Emotional Strength

Emotional strength is the capacity of a person to handle difficult situations – stressing and pressured scenarios – without a significant reduction in reasonable thinking. It is also the ability of a person to express the right emotion in accordance with the right setting. People who have tremendous emotional strength can navigate from a series of trials and obstacles without getting paralyzed by their situation. This is a key element to success. According to Sir Winston Churchill, *"Success is going from failure to failure without losing enthusiasm."*

If intellectual strength can be quantified using IQ, emotional strength can be measured using *Emotional Intelligence (EI)*, sometimes also called *Emotional Quotient (EQ)*. It is defined as the ability to identify and manage your emotions as well as the emotions of others. To have a *feel* of the level of your EQ, then try to answer honestly the following questions:

- When something bad happens, are you paranoid or calm? Are you prone to over-analyzing things or do you tend to look objectively as possible at your alternatives?
- When a person does something good to you, are you expressive or repressive?
- When a person is mad at you, do you have the tendency to retaliate or do you have the skill to calm yourself and the other person as well?

If your answers to those three questions lean more towards the positive side, then you can say that you have a strong EQ. However, if your answers are quite negative, then you need to work on your EQ. Develop it and one day you will be able to harness it and use it to your advantage.

3. Physical Strength

The most common and most visible of all strengths, physical strength, is the ability of an individual to perform challenging and daunting tasks that test the limits of the physical body. These tasks could include, but are not limited to, physical sports, demanding work such as lifting heavy items, and trying not to sleep or eat for several days. These activities are heavily taxing on the body, thus the term *"physical strength."*

Because the body consists of many different parts, there are also different ways to measure the overall physical strength of a person. A body builder in the gym might have the physical strength to lift heavy things such as a 200lb barbell, but at the same time, don't have the physical strength to run for 10 miles without getting fatigued.

To properly identify and determine your strengths, you need to categorize them into these three major categories. However, for a deeper understanding of how strength works for us and the boost it can provide in your journey towards self-improvement and development, then we will now go the next section.

Importance of Playing Inside your Strength Zone

Personal development guru, Paul Meyer, said, *"Focus on your strengths instead of your weaknesses, on your powers instead of your problems."* Playing inside your strength zone is one of the fastest ways to achieve your goals in life. However, most people have this wrong notion that they must focus their time to strengthen their weaknesses. Wrong. Let me illustrate it with a story.

There was a guy who lived on a mountain all his life. His livelihood consisted of planting crops and eating what they produced so he never had the need to go down to the village at the foot of the mountain. However, there were times when hikers would pass through his place and he welcomed them warmly. One day, he overheard them talking about some valuable coins that were hidden on the mountain. He learned that these coins were worth a fortune and could even buy the whole mountain where he lived.

A great interest to find those coins sparked in the guy's heart. So, the next morning, he set out to find them and after a few weeks of searching, he found the coins that the hikers were talking about. He took the bag of coins to his house and examined it. He noticed that there were two groups of coins; one was copper while the other was gold. He also noticed that the copper coins were dirty and tarnished. He thought to himself, *"Oh, these dirty coins must be cleansed first before I bring it to the village. For sure, its value will dramatically increase if I turn these tarnished coins into shiny ones."*

Focusing on your weaknesses, and exerting effort on them is like cleaning and shining the dirty copper coins in the hope that they will become more valuable. Sure, you can improve and be good at what you do, but as American athlete, Barry Bonds said, *"You either have it or you don't."* That is why it is crucial for any person to work insider their strength zone, because that is where excellence lies. It's the same with the story of Audubon; his escapades in his commercial ventures did not work out because he was playing his weaknesses.

Identifying your Personal Strengths

After establishing the importance of playing within your strength zone, it's time now to identify what those particular strengths you have. But before we do that, here are some additional benefits and advantages you can get once you identify your personal strength assets:

- It will be instrumental to your personal success.
- It could be your most powerful weapon to face life's adversity.
- It is your best way to impact society.
- It is your path to achieve self-actualization.

Now, going back to the principle of determining your strengths, it is vital you keep your eyes open when it comes to your progress in this aspect of your life. Discovering where you have strengths may seem like common sense, but believe me when I say that it is not. A lot of people still live a life that falls beneath their potential because they have failed to discover this one simple truth. In the words of Marilyn Vos Sayant, *"Success is achieved by developing our strengths, not by eliminating our weaknesses."* So, to help you in identifying your personal strengths, consider this advice:

1. Take A Personal Assessment Test

The trickiest part of identifying your strengths is discounting what you can really do while overestimating what you can't do. Do you know people like that? They have great confidence and eagerness to do some things in which they do not really excel.

At the same time, you can see how good they are in doing other things, but they seem oblivious of that fact. Taking a personal assessment of your strengths is one way to avoid this.

There are a lot of organizations and resources online that help you in evaluating yourself in terms of your strengths. Gallup's StrengthsFinder 2.0 is one of those resources that lets you identify the areas where you are strong. The test is simple. After buying their book, you can access the private examination online using an encrypted key. Based on your answers, the algorithm will give you your top five strengths that you need to focus on.

Taking these kinds of personal assessments is the fastest way to get an idea of your personal strengths. However, answer the questions truthfully to the best of your ability, speak about what's really happening and not your ideal scenario, and lastly, do not forget to get feedback from people closest to you to determine the accuracy of your test results.

2. Evaluate Your Past Years

If you want more actual insights about your personal strengths, then go over the past years and past decades and evaluate your previous experiences. Our experiences in the past paint a canvass of who we are and what things we are very good at. Perhaps the idea might seem abstract to you right now, but let me help you in doing it. Try to answer the following questions by remembering your past experiences:

- Is there an activity that you were doing before and upon finishing it, you constantly received praise and acknowledgment from other people?

- What are the most common kinds of problems encountered by your friends that they ask your opinion about?

- What are those things that you can do without exerting too much effort compared to the effort given by your friends?

- What are those activities that you enjoyed a lot?

These questions are not conclusive. However, it can stimulate your thinking to go back to your past experiences and evaluate yourself considering your personal strengths. Remember this: if it is your strength, you can easily do it (compared to others), you are getting recognition because of it, and your opinion is valued in that specific subject.

3. Assess yourself and validate your results with the people closest to you

After evaluating your past experiences, you can also look to your current life and answer the same set of questions. This section requires you to reflect deep within yourself and evaluate each possible scenario that exemplifies your personal strengths. Perhaps you consistently provide valuable insights about the different aspects of the operation of your company. Maybe, you speak in a way that people cannot help but to listen to you. Or maybe, you have this eye to see the future, can clearly see what you want to accomplish and how other people can contribute to it.

Get a piece of paper and write down all the possible strengths you can think about. On the opposite side, write down a scenario where this strength is exhibited. List as many scenarios as possible because it will give you an insight into those things you are good at. After doing this, talk with two to three people that know you best and discuss with them the personal assessment you have done. Ask for an honest opinion and do not fish for compliments. Remember, the goal here is to identify your strengths and not to boost your ego.

There are a lot of other ways to determine and zero in on your personal strengths. However, these three suggestions can get you started in evaluating yourself and identifying what you are good at in the process. Also, please note that finding your strengths takes time. In fact, it could take years for some people. Therefore, be patient. If you have a lot of time, do some experimentation and if you are quite busy, set aside a specific time of the day to explore a strength you have identified.

Developing Your Strengths

Identifying your strengths is not enough; you must also invest your time in cultivating and developing them. The Father of Modern Management, Peter Drucker, said, *"Use feedback analysis to identify your strengths. Then go to work on improving your strengths. Identify and eliminate bad habits that hinder the full development of your strengths. Figure out what you should do and do it. Finally, decide what you should not do."*

Developing and building on what you are good at is as crucial as finding your strengths. If you have determined your craft, but you do not capitalize on it, then every effort you have exerted in finding it will be wasted. It's like the traveler who went on a journey of a thousand miles just to reach the city of London, just to miss his hometown and return to it immediately. If you are serious in improving yourself, then take time to develop your strengths. Here's how:

1. Develop One to Two Strengths at a Time

In the previous section of this chapter, I elaborated that our strengths can be divided and further sub-divided into different categories. Though most of these strengths are complementary to each other, trying to develop everything all at once will be a losing battle. Multi-tasking won't work when it comes to developing your strengths. Though it is important to polish your tools, utilizing the power of focus is also vital.

If you could identify your strengths using the principles in the previous sections, then I would challenge you to pick one to two strengths. Also, it would help if you can rank your strength and arrange it in a pattern. For instance, if you recognize that you have the intellectual strength to understand what you are learning, and you also have the strength to communicate clearly to other people, then focus first on building your knowledge. In that way, when you try to communicate to other people, you can provide more clarity since you will already know what to speak to them about.

Don't be overwhelmed by the task. Instead, see every step as necessary in building your ammunition and preparing to become the very best version of yourself. Developing your strengths is a lifetime process, so there is no need to hurry.

2. Gather Resources to Sharpen You

One of the best ways to develop your strengths is to learn from people who have already done what you want to accomplish. That's the reason why you need to gather resources – books, audio tapes, videos – that will teach you the practices applied by already successful people. Remember this: you can't grow on your own. A plant will not grow to maturity if it is isolated in a dark room with no sunlight and water.

You might have heard that smart people learn from their experiences. But I say, people who learn from the experiences of others are way smarter. The stories of the authors that are written in the pages of their book are a valuable gold mine that will teach you great lessons in life. And if you take the time to read every day, then there is no saying what you can achieve in future years to come. As Charles "Tremendous" Jones said, *"You will be the same person in five years as you are today except for the people you meet and the books you read."*

3. Apply. Practice. Mastery.

You need to consistently sharpen your skills if you are to develop and build on your strengths. This might be the most challenging part of developing yourself. Let's face it: most of us are good starters but never great finishers. Reading a book is not enough. Listening to audio tapes is not enough. Watching great speakers is not enough.

If you want to develop and cultivate your strengths, then you need to continuously apply everything that you have learned. Practice it and try to improve on it by learning new things, system, and techniques. After a lot of practice, one day, you will master your strength.

"Each person is intuitively designed with a unique strength for a unique service on Earth. It's your responsibility to find your strength and unleash the possibilities within you" – Chindah Chindah

Tony Robbins, the life and transformational coach said, *"It's not what we do once in a while that shapes our lives. It's what we do consistently."* Aristotle, the philosopher echoes the same sentiment. He said, *"We are what we repeatedly do. Excellence, then, is not an act, but a habit."* If you want to eat the fruit, then nurture the tree. In the same way, if you want to experience the benefits of excellence, then keep nurturing yourself. Never stop learning. Make growing yourself through developing your strength an indispensable part of yourself.

Discussion Questions and Reflections:

This portion of each chapter aims to establish the concepts and principles that you learned so far. Try to carefully consider each question and answer it with complete reflection on how it applies to your life. I would also implore you to take notes and even share what you have learned to others to initiate healthy discussion.

1. Before reading this chapter, what comes to your mind when you hear the word,"*strength?*" How does your perception of that word shape how you view yourself and the journey of success? After learning the truth about strength, why do you think it is essential in a person's life?

_____

_____

_____

2. Have you already identified your strengths? In the three categories of strengths, namely, *intellectual, emotional, and physical,* what category most suits you? What about your weaknesses? How are you coping with those things that you don't do well?

_____

_____

_____

3. Have you already taken the steps outlined in this chapter to help you identify your strengths? Write down the summary and results of your personal assessment here. Also, identify experiences in the past that exemplify the area you are especially good at. What about the feedback of people closest to you? Is your self-assessment consistent with how they see you in terms of your strengths? Why or why not?

_____

_____

4. How do you develop your strengths? When was the last time that you picked up a book with the aim to improve what you know? Why do you think improving and developing your strengths are crucial steps in self-improvement? What are the benefits you can get once you take the challenge of continuous personal development seriously?

_____

_____

_____

THE ROAD LESS TRAVELLED

CHAPTER 4

*"How can I go forward when I don't
know which way I'm facing?"*

— *John Lennon*

The process of personal growth and self-improvement doesn't really ring a bell for a lot of people. For them, it is better to continue climbing the ladder of success in their careers while increasing the digits in their bank accounts. These people think that while it is important to improve yourself, there are a whole lot of other urgent matters that must be prioritized over personal development. They act as if the two are mutually exclusive choices, but the sad fact is they have chosen those things that they consider urgent and left the important aspect of self-improvement on the back burner all their lives.

"Personal growth is a choice you must make if you want more from your life" – Chindah Chindah

This kind of thinking is more harmful than helpful. The previous chapters established the need for change and how to effect change in your life. We also discussed the importance of discovering your strengths and improving them. Even an average person will agree that these things are vital for success, therefore, in this chapter, we will zoom in in more detail about how we can bridge the gap from our current location to our desired destination in this life.

As we continuously embark on the journey towards success, you will realize that most of the things you need are already within you. All you must do is to take out your toolbox and use it to move along the path to self-improvement – the road less travelled.

The Great Separator

The story of renowned leadership expert Dr. John C. Maxwell is a great example of an individual who chose the road less travelled. Right now, you will know him as a leadership expert who was able to train millions of leaders worldwide. He has also authored almost 70 books on topics related to personal growth and development particularly in the aspect of leadership, communication, and potential. He has already sold more than 25 million books and his work has been translated in different languages.

In addition to this, Dr. Maxwell is also a recipient of different recognitions and awards, including being named as the most influential leadership expert in the world by *Business Insider* and *Inc. Magazine*. Also, for six consecutive years, he has been voted as the top leadership professional in the world on Leadership Gurus. Dr. Maxwell has also founded five companies.

Now, you might think he has always been successful, but you would be wrong. John C. Maxwell started out just like each one of us. However, he was blessed to have parents who valued personal growth and self-improvement. John used to tell the story of how his father would pay him and his brother a small amount of money just to read books.

This activity helped him develop a lifelong commitment to learning. John's parents also showed him the value of finding the right friends and his father modelled to him the importance of living a life in service to others. His father also regularly brought him to different seminars to hear great speakers.

John's father paved the way, but he was still the one to choose to walk it. Even in his younger years, John already had a sense of what he wanted to do with the rest of his life. But what separated John from his pals was his awareness of the importance of learning and personal development. That's why several years after graduating, John was able to stand apart from his contemporaries and recognized as an authority in the area of leadership. And as they say, the rest is history.

If you are aspiring to achieve more in your life and accomplish a lot of great things like Dr. Maxwell, then you need to embrace the importance of personal growth and development in your life. It is my personal conviction that all individuals have a well of unlimited potential within them. However, the magnitude and the degree to how you use it to propel you towards success are highly determined by your willingness to commit yourself to growth and self-improvement. You need to have the courage to choose and walk towards the path of the road less travelled, and this chapter will teach you how to do exactly that.

The Three-Pronged Approach

To ascertain the required learning pathway that you need to arrive at your destination, we need to firmly establish three particular aspects of your life. I call this the *"Three-Pronged Approach."* First, we need to establish and evaluate your past experiences. There are powerful lessons that are scattered among the seemingly-random stuff that happened in your past. While there are probably several significant events that have transpired, at the same time there are also routine things that have been a part of your life ever since. Second, we ascertain and assess your current situation. Every realistic plan to achieve a goal involves the need to pinpoint the exact location that we are in. If you want to go from point A to point B, then you need to determine first, where point A really is. Lastly, we will discuss the steps that you can take to bridge the gap from where you are right now, to the place you want to go.

However, the *Three-Pronged Approach* poses serious challenges. First, in evaluating your past experiences, we need to properly establish the lessons as objectively as possible. If we are honest, we all have some mistakes that occur in a revolving cycle in our lives. Normally, we blame other people, the circumstances around it, or even random chances why those mistakes happen. But if we truly want to obtain the lessons surrounding it, then you need to take responsibility for everything that happens in your life.

Don't be like the clumsy driver who always blamed others. One day he was involved in a series of minor road skirmishes. After colliding with another car, he angrily opened the door of his vehicle and bolted out to confront the other driver. He shouted, *"What's wrong with you people?! Don't you look down the road when you are driving? You're the fourth person who has crashed with me today!"* Every time we see *the* problem as belonging to someone else, then that kind of thinking is the problem.

Another issue of the *Three-Pronged Approach* is having heavily tinted glasses. Depending on our personalities, we might see our current situation as much better than the real situation, or we might look at ourselves and think we are worse than what we truly are. To address this challenge, we can always ask for validation from people who are genuinely close to and concerned for us to confirm our personal assessment.

Evaluating Your Past Experiences

Author Jim Butcher wisely commented, *"It was never too late to learn something. The past is unalterable in any event. The future is the only thing we can change. Learning the lessons of the past is the only way to shape the present and the future."* This quotation summarizes the need to learn from what happened yesterday. Though, I agree that dwelling too much on the past won't do you any good in the future, there are still some lessons that are written in the history of your life that can teach you valuable lessons. As philosopher and novelist, George Santayana, said, *"Those who cannot remember the past are condemned to repeat it."*

If you want to be a student of yourself and learn from your past, then identify and consider these two major things that have happened in your life:

1. The Greatest Trials

Our lives are composed of a series of problems. If you don't have any problem right now, then it could only mean two things: first, you will soon have a problem; or second, you are already dead. Trials and challenges are part of our daily lives. In fact, no one can escape it. It doesn't matter if you are the richest man in the world or the poorest beggar living under the bridge; if you are in this world, you will have problems.

John Maxwell said, *"Three reasons problems are inevitable; first, we live in a world of growing complexity; second, we interact with people; and third, we cannot control all the situation we face."* Within this reasoning, we can come up with two general categories of problems: those that result from our wrong decisions and those that are outside our control.

For instance, being regularly late in your office can get you into trouble. You can be subjected to warnings from your HR Department that can cause you a lot of stress. Your attitude of being consistently late will also reduce your pay and can cost you your job as well. Now, the reason you are late is an entirely different matter. And here's where the category of control comes in. If the reason is because you're always waking up late, then your problem is within your circle of control. However, if you are late because of extraordinary events that happen while you are going to work, such as vehicle accidents and natural calamity, then you can do nothing about it.

Now, I would like you to look back at your past and try to identify the major trials and problems you have undergone. Try to narrow down your list to those vital problems that alter the normal life you have. This problem might cost you a lot of money, it might also cause you tremendous stress in the past, or break some of your important relationships. List down those trials as we evaluate your past in light of these peculiar problems. After that, consider the following questions:

a. What is the cause of your trials?

As I have mentioned earlier, our problems can be a result of factors that are within our control or outside our control. Again, we can do nothing about those things that we can't control. Blaming yourself for the event that did not materialize because of bad weather will do you no good. Therefore, in this question, I want you to come up with the causes that are within the circle of your control.

Why did you fail in your business endeavor? Why did you cut ties with some friends? Why was your son angry at you? Think about those causes and if you identify that the trials are a direct result of your mistake, then kindly take note. This process is vital to be able to glean the lessons from your past trials. As Harold J. Smith once said, *"More people would learn from their mistakes if they weren't so busy denying them."*

b. What is the actual trial?

Describe in as vivid detail as possible the trials that you have identified. Paint the scenario, the circumstances, the emotions that you felt and the people that were affected by them. After identifying the cause of these problems, it is also crucial to understand in greater depth the bad results of the mistake. What are the difficult emotions that you felt while undergoing the trial? Are you angry and resentful? Do you feel a terrible sense of guilt? How about the people around you? Were they in pain too?

Understanding the trial is important because it shows you the consequence that your mistakes can make in your life. Writer, Sherrilyn Kenyon quipped, *"It's easy to make mistakes. It's living with the consequences of them that's the hardest."*

c. What is your response to the trial?

After identifying the cause of the problem and remembering the consequences of your mistakes, the next thing that you need to do is to evaluate your response to the problem. By knowing the patterns of your responses, you can clearly identify if what you do contributes to solving the problem, or if it makes the matters worse and more complicated.

This scenario is typical for most people. After committing some serious mistakes, they will do their best to hide it to other people. The person who is at fault will create a web of lies just to make sure that the wrong he did will not be found out by other individuals. However, in the process of lying and hiding the truth, a series of bigger mistakes will be committed and will leave the person in misery.

Also, our response to trials can also cause these trials to repeat themselves. For instance, if you know that eating sweets will trigger a searing headache and yet you continuously consume large amounts of chocolates, ice cream, and sweets regularly, then you can expect that the trial of headaches will keep repeating.

How did you respond to the trials that you identified? Did you change yourself for the better because of it or do your best just to avoid further consequences of that specific problem? Did you ask for help from your closest friends or try to solve it on your own and break down in the process?

By contemplating your past trials, you can come up with several lessons that these experiences want to teach you. Identifying the mistakes that you committed, the consequences that you needed to face, and the actual response that you made will also provide you with the answers you can use to face any future problems that come your way.

Learn from it but don't repeat it. As Albert Einstein once said, *"Insanity is doing the same thing, over and over again, but expecting different results."*

2. Your Greatest Victories

As much as your past problems can teach you a lot about yourself, your past victories also provide you with a wealth of information that you can use to improve you and your current situation. If your past trials can give you insights about the things that you did wrong, your past wins can give you some awareness about the things that you did right. Both are essential to your journey towards success.

Though I must admit that I believe our failures can teach us infinitely more things than our victories can, it is still crucial to take note of the things we are doing right to establish the process of duplication. Here are the things you need to consider in evaluating your past victories:

a. What you did right?

The moment you could achieve a specific goal, or you were able to accomplish an amazing feat, will lead you to a realization you have done something right. If you are just beginning in your journey to success, then you will realize some attempts are more successful than others. Now, if you are wise enough to learn from yourself, you must know that those things that give you the results you want must be repeated.

Author, Robert Collier, asserted, *"Success is the sum of small efforts, repeated day in and day out."* The truth is success is just an outcome of the daily actions that you take. If reading a lot of books increases your wisdom, then do more of it. If talking to people with a broader mindset helps you to develop more positive thinking, then do more of it. Whenever you see an activity is helping you to achieve more success, then make sure that you do more of it.

b. What are the elements of your victory?

For most people, their victories are not just a result of taking solo courageous efforts. On the contrary, their successes in life have been achieved with the help of people around them, the actions that they did, and the opportunities that they took. To think that you became successful because of yourself is both ignorant and dangerous.

Entrepreneur, Reid Hoffman, said, *"No matter how brilliant your mind or strategy, if you're playing a solo game, you'll always lose out to a team."* The first element of a person's victory is other people. Whether it's the author of the book that he usually reads, or his friends on the side line that offers encouragement, help from other people is always needed to be successful.

The second element of victory is your best effort. No matter how much push you receive from your companions, no matter how much wisdom you glean from a book, and no matter how many opportunities were offered to you, if you won't go out there and take action, then you won't be victorious. Taking action is at the heart of the success journey. People who work continuously towards their goal are most likely to achieve them. That is the plain truth of success.

The last element of victory is the opportunities that you take.

Now, there is a common misconception when it comes to success. Most people think that opportunities come only on special occasions. Therefore, they wait for them. However, as Thomas Edison said, *"Opportunity is missed by most people because it is dressed in overalls and looks like work."* Look back at your victories and you will realize these things happened for you because you decided to take the opportunities presented to you, or you opted to create your own opportunity.

c. *What are the lessons you learned?*

There is no success that happen to anyone without a cost. For most individuals, their success is just a result of unwavering perseverance and purposeful stubbornness. In fact, there is no shortcut to success. This principle is also true of your past victories. To learn from what your previous accomplishments, you need to ask yourself the following questions:

- What character was developed in me in achieving this victory?
- What are the specific lessons that this success taught me?
- What experiences helped me achieve my goals? Is it worth it?

Failures and success are inseparable. They are two sides of the same coin. Your victories and losses are both part of a journey that will take you higher in your destination in life. Though failures can teach us more about our lives compared to success, I believe you can still learn by succeeding in life. Winning can teach you the value of other people and help you develop the character of gratitude. Victories can teach you that anything is possible if you put your heart in what you do. In all of this, one thing is certain, if you want to improve your current situation, you need to learn from both your past trials and past victories.

Assessing Your Current Situation

After dealing with the past, now it's time to go back to the present and do a careful assessment of your current situation. Technically speaking, your present is the only time that you can directly influence. The past is already over so you can't do anything about it. Your future is yet to come and there's no guarantee you will ever face it, so it's pointless to worry about it. Today is the only day that you can influence and whatever you do today can help you shape your tomorrow.

Chinese Philosopher Lao Tzu said it even better. He said, "*If you are depressed, you are living in the past. If you are anxious, you are living in the future. If you are at peace, you are living in the present.*"

In order to arrive at your desired destination, then you must be certain of what your current location is. It's like the neophyte traveler who wants to climb a mountain. After two hours of walking in the woods, he realized he was not getting closer to the mountain where he wanted to go. So, he sat for a moment on a nearby rock and ate his lunch. While eating the lunch that he'd prepared earlier in the morning, a local villager passed by. The traveler greeted him accordingly, showed the map and asked, "*I've been walking for almost two hours to get to that mountain, but instead of getting nearer, I realized that I'm actually getting farther from it. Can you help me?*" The local villager smiled and softly said, "*Sir, I'm sorry, but you cannot get to that mountain from here. You need to go to this place,*" while pointing at a specific point on the map, "*to get there.*"

If you don't know where you are right now, it's hard to chart a course to get to the place that you want to go. To help you in assessing your current situation, then I encourage you to focus on these three important areas of your life: your current skills, your current thoughts and your current goals.

1. Your current skills

Any realistic personal assessment must take note of the current skill level that a person has. Any organization knows that's why there are interviews that applicants need to go through before being employed by a company. Without proper assessment of your current skills, it's hard to determine the training and activities you still need to go through to achieve your dream.

Ralph Waldo Emerson said, *"Wherever we go, whatever we do, self is the sole subject we study and learn."* To help you in doing a simple personal assessment of your current skills, answer the following questions:

a. What is your educational background?

Your educational background gives you an idea of the things that you already know. If you are still taking your undergraduate degree, then no one expects you to have doctoral degree. Also, your educational background provides a realistic evaluation of the level of expertise that you have.

For instance, if you are aiming to become a great doctor and you're still finishing your pre-med degree, then you already have a clear idea of the road that you need to take. By knowing where you currently are in terms of your education, then it is easier to know what the knowledge, skills, and experience still needed to gain to become a doctor.

b. What is your employment background?

This is also straightforward. Though the academic background of a person might probably be in line for the career he will choose, this is not always entirely the case. Your employment background can be a more accurate measure of your current expertise regardless of the educational background you have. If you have finished a degree in accounting, then spend several years as a writer, people can expect you to be a more expert writer than an expert accountant.

Also, during employment, an individual slowly discovers the things she really wants to do. If you have been employed for a considerable number of years, then you know what I am talking about.

c. What is your strength zone?

Unlike the first two areas of skills, your strength zone is not that easy to determine. Assessing and identifying the strength of a person has always been a challenge because the evidence supporting it might not always be obvious. To be honest, assessing your personal strengths could require an entire book or course of its own, so I can't provide you the exact steps to determine it in your life.

Besides, there are a whole lot of resources that you can find online that can give you the answers to this aspect of your skills. Just remember, as Napoleon Hill said, *"Strength and growth come only through continuous effort and struggle."* One way to discover your strength is to try doing different things and be aware of those activities where you naturally excel.

2. Your current thoughts

Craig Groeschel, the senior pastor of Life Church, once said, *"Your life is moving in the direction of your strongest thoughts."* After that bold declaration, he asked a piercing question, *"Are you excited where your thoughts are taking you?"* If there is one thing that is responsible for how we see the world, how we respond to what's happening to us, and how we live our lives, it is our minds. The way our mind works determines our outlook on life, our behaviors and attitude, and even the minutest detail of every decision we make.

That's why our mind is the greatest battlefield. Before we win a single battle in the physical realm, a war is being waged in the recess of our mind. Your thoughts must be in check if you want to go from point A to point B. Albert Einstein explained the importance of this by saying, *"We can't solve problems by using the same kind of thinking we used when we created them."* Therefore, in assessing your thoughts, ask yourself the following questions:

a. Are your thoughts more positive or negative?

There were two applicants who were both applying for the same job. They had both graduated from a prestigious university with honors. Neither had any work experience, but they were skilled, intelligent, and capable. However, one trait that separated them was the way they thought. You see, the first applicant displayed a high level of optimism while the second one was mostly pessimistic in the way he saw things.

Both talked to themselves while waiting for their interview. The pessimistic applicant said to himself, "*My gosh. I'm not prepared for this. I'm really nervous. What if I fail the interview? I can't stop myself from shaking because of fear. It's my first time, and I'm quite sure I will fail this.*" However, the optimistic guy thought to himself, "*My gosh! This is it! I've been preparing for this my whole life. I'm so excited! What if I pass the interview? I can't stop myself from smiling because of the thrill of being accepted in my first job application. It's my first time, I know, but I'm confident that I will pull this off!*"

Now, who do you think will be given the job? It's easier to see when put that way, right? Yet, for most people, they cannot see the harm that negative thinking brings to their lives. A little worrying here, a bit of anxiousness there, and a pint of pessimism in every activity, and we have the complete recipe for a miserable life. So, let me ask you this question:

On a scale of 1 to 10, rate the way you have thought for the past week. If your thoughts were highly positive, meaning, you generally saw the good in every situation and you expected the best results from your endeavors, then you can give yourself a score of 10. However, if your thoughts were highly negative, meaning, you expected the worst to happen and you always thought critically of the people around you, then rate yourself lower.

1 2 3 4 5 6 7 8 9 10

After rating your thought life in terms of positivity and negativity, identify the particular reasons why you tended to think this way. If you are not satisfied with the results of your thought assessment, then what actions do you need to start taking today?

b. *What are your persistent thoughts?*

The idea of persistent thoughts is evaluating your mind to see those patterns of thinking that continually reveal themselves in your everyday life. Perhaps, you are consistently being bothered by the business that you want to start, but you are afraid to do so. Or maybe you always find yourself thinking about the mistakes that you did in the past and you are fearful if somebody finds out.

Your persistent thoughts are important because they can help you to drive faster towards destination success or lead you down the road of destination failure. Remember, the more you think of something, the more it will control your life. Now, it all depends on what you are always thinking about. If you are continually pondering the potential you have and how you can employ it in your journey, then that's good. However, if you are continually being fearful of the possibility of failing, then you need to change those persistent thoughts immediately.

c. *How is your thinking changing your life?*

Henry Ford said, *"Whether you think you can, or you can't – either way you're right."* Notice that the results of your endeavor are a function of the way you think. Going back to the earlier example of the two neophyte applicants, why do we instinctively know that the optimistic applicant will be accepted? The answer is that deep in our being, we all have this awareness that our thinking contributes largely to the way we live our lives. In short, if we think we can, we can and if we think we can't, then we really can't.

I would like you to spend a few minutes to reflect on your state of thinking these past few days. How does your thinking change your life?

How does your pattern of thoughts affect your response to circumstances and people around you? Is the way your mind works being helpful or does it just contribute to makes matters worst? In your own words, I would like you to write down the effect thinking can have to a person's life.

This is most vital because if our lives are being shaped by the way we think, then we need to take immediate action and responsibility to guard our thoughts. It's hard to go to our desired destination if we are still thinking in terms of our current location. Let me illustrate this point with an analogy:

Imagine yourself going to another country that has an entirely different culture, customs, values, and philosophies compared to your native land. However, you don't have a choice but to go to this country and build your life there. You surmise that in order to succeed in your new life in this new country, you need to understand their culture and befriend your new neighbors. It's hard considering that all your life has been spent in your native land. Now, do you think that you will succeed if you would still live according to the culture, customs, values and philosophies of your native land? No. Instinctively we know you need to adapt if you want to survive.

It's the same thing with our thinking. If we want to climb new heights in our career, if we want to level up in the things that we undertake, if we want to achieve more success in our lives, then we need also to transform ourselves by changing the way we think. It's the only way forward and underscores the importance of assessing your current thoughts of life.

3. Your current goals

A new mountaineer decided to conquer Mt. Everest within two years. However, since he was just a beginner, he knew it would take a lot of training, guts, and grit to accomplish his ultimate goal. So, after some careful deliberation, he talked to a few people who had already climbed the highest mountain in the world. He inquired of the regiments that they undertook, the diet that they consumed, and the disciplines they employed to make the climb possible.

After a month of interviewing these other mountain climbers, he had an entire list of things he had to do to achieve his goal. However, upon coming home, he decided to discard all those tips and advice. He still wanted to climb Everest within two years, but he realized he wanted to prepare for his goal by finishing all the video games that he'd bought last week and spent two years doing so. Now, do you think that he will still be able to achieve his goal of conquering the Mt. Everest? Absolutely, no.

It's the same thing with us. If our current goals are not in accordance with accomplishing our larger goals, then we can't arrive at our desired destination. Evaluating your current goals is essential to establish a learning pathway to achieve your life goals. Someone once said, *"Ask yourself if what you're doing today is getting you closer to where you want to be tomorrow."* In the same way, ask yourself if your current goals are helping you to go closer to what you want to accomplish in the near future. To help you in doing that, answer the following questions:

1. *What are your short-term goals?*

Short-term goals pertain to those things that you want to achieve within one year or less. Because of the time frame of these goals, then they could also be considered *"urgent goals"* or something you must achieve immediately. Normally, short-term goals are easier to achieve but still challenging enough to push you to level-up in different aspects of your life.

Also, using the S-M-A-R-T method, as detailed below, will help you to properly evaluate the goals you are setting for yourself. To help you in using this method, kindly answer the following questions:

1. **Is your goal Specific enough?** Do you have the exact definition of your target? For instance, losing weight is too broad a goal, but if you detail you want to lose a minimum of 20lbs then it becomes specific.

2. **Is your goal Measurable?** Your goal must have a quantifiable quantity to track your progress or determine if you have actually achieved it. Like in the example above, 20lbs is the measure of the goal. It will also help if you affix a deadline on when you must achieve this.

3. **Is your goal Attainable?** Your goal must be challenging enough to push you to try harder, but not impossible to accomplish that will drive you to just give up. It is always based on your own assessment. If 20lbs represents a number that gives you a challenge, yet is also attainable by exerting extra effort, then it can be considered attainable.

4. **Is your goal Relevant?** Why do you want to achieve it? What does it mean for you if you lose weight? Your goal must not also be tied up with other people. It must connect with you

on a profound and personal level for it to be considered relevant.

5. **Is your goal Time-bound?** "Someday" and "next month" cannot be found in the calendar and therefore you can't use them for your goals either. Your goal must have an exact date to create a sense of urgency within you.

Use your time to assess your short-term goals and evaluate your plans in accordance with the great things you want to accomplish. Tony Robbins once said, *"Setting goals is the first step in turning the invisible into the visible."* See the visible short-term victories so you can find confidence to shoot for bigger things.

2. *What are your long-term goals?*

If there are short-term goals, then there are also goals that can be considered long-term. These are goals that you want to achieve within five to 10 years or longer. Basically, the entire concept discussed above is also applicable to long-term goals. However, what makes these goals more challenging is the longer period of waiting that you need to endure. And this is where perseverance and persistence enters the picture.

Most people get lost in the realm of doing and achieving that they forget the importance of developing themselves as they achieve their goals.

As Henry David Thoreau said, *"What you get by achieving your goals is not as important as what you become by achieving your goals."* What matters most in the discipline of goal setting is not the goal itself but the transformation that the process of getting it will bring to your life.

If there is one thing that can show you the path you are about to take, it is your current goals. Assessing and evaluating the suitability of it to your overall life plan is vital to get from here to there. So, make sure you set aside some time to reflect on your goals and be prepared to do any adjustments if necessary.

Bridging the Gap

After carefully evaluating your past experiences and the current situation in life, now you must be prepared to do any necessary steps to bridge the gap. The key word here that will help you to accomplish this feat is *"discipline."* Jim Rohn said, *"Discipline is the bridge between goals and accomplishment."* In the same way, discipline is the bridge to connect you from your current location and the destination that you want to reach. Here are four important disciplines you must cultivate to bridge the gap:

1. The Discipline of Guarding Your Mind

As I have mentioned earlier, our mind is the most crucial battleground we need to win. Lose it and you also lose your chance to change your life. If you will continuously dwell on thoughts of defeatism and negativities, I guarantee that you will wind down the road of misery. Business magnate, Tony Robbins, shared the same sentiment he learnt from his mentor. He said, *"My teacher Jim Rohn taught me a simple principle: every day, stand guard at the door of your mind, and you alone decide what thoughts and beliefs you let into your life. For they will shape whether you feel rich or poor, cursed or blessed."*

Guarding your mind is not easy especially if we have conditioned ourselves to believe the pessimistic outcomes of everything. We need to flush out all those negative thoughts and replace them with optimistic and positive thoughts. This principle might be difficult at first, but doing some minor adjustments in your life can do the trick. Try to write positive statements on small cards that you can carry anywhere and constantly refer to during the day.

2. The Discipline of Daily Self-Improvement

Don't let any day pass by without learning anything new. Your everyday goal must become a little better than yesterday. Golfer and broadcaster, Ken Venturi, once said, *"I don't believe you have to be better than everybody else. I believe you have to be better than **your** every thought could be."* Commit yourself to constant self-improvement and set aside a specific time of the day to do your personal development habits.

One thing that consistently comes up when talking about the principle of self-improvement is reading books. In fact, people throughout the ages have expressed the same sentiment. Socrates said, *"Employ your time in improving yourself by other men's writings, so that you shall gain easily what others have labored hard for."* Dr. Seuss quipped, *"The more you read, the more things you will know. The more that you learn, the more places you'll go."* And lastly, Jim Rohn warned, *"The only thing worse than not reading a book in the last ninety days is not reading a book in the last ninety days and thinking that it doesn't matter."*

Be a student of life. Learn a little bit of something every day and before you know it, you are a changed person. To implement this discipline in your life, craft a portion of your schedule and set it aside solely for reading. Try to finish one book a month and learn from the wisdom of people who have already achieved the success that you have.

3. The Discipline of Goal Setting and Goal Getting

I have emphasized earlier the importance of identifying your current goals. However, if you are like the average person, I would assume you don't really have a clear goal for your life. Most people don't set goals and live on a hit and miss basis. When they hit something, they gladly celebrate and call it their goal. But is it? J.P. Morgan asserted, *"The first step towards getting somewhere is to decide that you are not going to stay where you are."* You do that by setting clear goals for your life.

I already taught you the S-M-A-R-T method that you can use to assess your goals. However, to make sure you increase your odds in achieving your goals, then consider the following tips:

a. Write it down. Author, Brian Tracy, said, *"People with clear, written goals, accomplish far more in a shorter period than people without them could ever imagine."*

b. Make it a habit to review your goals consistently. Les Brown, an American motivational speaker quipped, *"Review your goals twice every day to be focused on achieving them."*

c. In order to get your goals, you must put your effort in achieving it.

Yes, there's no other way. Walt Disney, an American film producer asserted, *"The way to get started is to quit talking and begin doing."*

Dwayne Johnson, an American Actor insightfully said, *"The first step to achieving your goal is to take a moment to respect your goal. Know what it means to you to achieve it."* My friend, you have unlimited potential lying inside you and the best way to unleash that is to start setting goals for your life and do your best to achieve them.

4. The Discipline of Moving Forward in Your Life

If there is one thing that poses the greatest challenge when it comes to changing your life, it's our tendency to start and stop in the middle of the process. A lot of people quit at the faintest hint of trials and hardships. We cannot tolerate the obstacles when we try to go against the flow. However, that is the essence of change. If you are not encountering resistance, then you are not still in the pathway of change. Henry Ford insightfully commented, *"When everything seems to be going against you, remember that the airplane takes off against the wind, not with it."*

You must choose to move forward no matter what. Don't let the trials, hardships, and difficulties determine your destination. The path to success is always uphill. If there is one fear that you should nurture, it is the fear of staying the same all the days of your life. If you encounter struggle on the way to your desired destination, then remember the words of Scottish author and government reformer, Samuel Smiles:

"The battle of life is, in most cases, fought uphill; and to win it without a struggle were perhaps to win it without honor. If there were no difficulties there would be no success; if there were nothing to struggle for, there would be nothing to be achieved."

Indeed, it's the Road Less Travelled!

"The practice of self-discipline is hard but the reward is tangible and visible" – Chindah Chindah

Ascertaining the required learning pathway and choosing to walk on it is one of the biggest decisions you could make in your life. However, as you have seen in this chapter, most people will opt to stay where they currently are. They are people who opt to stay in their comfort zone and are too afraid to risk their cozy little space in their bubble world. Indeed, choosing the path of change and deciding to walk in it is the road less travelled. I cannot guarantee a stress-free ride, but just like Robert Frost said, *"I took the road less traveled by, and that has made all the difference."*

Discussion Questions and Reflections:

This portion of each chapter aims to establish the concepts and principles that you have learned so far. Try to carefully consider each question and answer it with a complete reflection of how it applies to your life. I would also implore you to take notes and even share what you have learned with others to initiate healthy discussion.

1. Based on your assessment of your current situation, what area of your life needs the most improvement? How do you see your current self? What aspects of your personality and character need total overhauling?

    _____

    _____

    _____

    _____

2. Do you have a clear idea of what your strengths are? What are those things that you can do naturally well? What are those things that give you higher return compared to other activities? Why do you think it is important to determine the set of skills and strength of a person? What is the difference that it can make to someone's life when he has a profound awareness of what he does best?

    _____

    _____

    _____

3. What aspects of your past have the most significant impact on your life? Highlight both positive and negative experiences that you have. Do you regret any of the decisions you have made before? If you had the power to go back in time, what is that one mistake you would like to correct?

If you can't go back in time, how have your experiences shaped the person that you are right now?

_____

_____

_____

_____

THE POWER OF CONSISTENCY

CHAPTER 5

"Success is all about consistency around the fundamentals."

– Robin Sharma

If there is one thing that will help you to get to your goals faster and get you to your desired destination earlier, it is taking steady and consistent actions daily. You can set big goals, think all the positive thoughts you want, and learn everything there is to learn. However, all these efforts will be wasted if there is no commitment to consistent actions on your end. One of the greatest prime ministers of England, Winston Churchill, said, *"Continuous effort – not strength or intelligence – is the key to unlocking your potential."* If you want to accomplish more of your goals, then there is no other way but to be consistent in what you do.

"A high-performance life is a life of higher level of consistency in what you are committed to achieve" – Chindah Chindah

However, despite this truth, being consistent is still one of the constant struggles of most individuals. A lot of people are so good in starting yet do not have the tenacity to stay in the process, especially during hard times. We have all experienced this in different points in our lives.

When we learn something new, or we hear a motivational speaker, or we have a pressing problem, we have no choice but to move. These things can spark actions and steps forward towards change. Yet, when the excitement fades, when the initial motivation loses its power and the pain has lessened, we stop midway in what we truly want to do. Businessman and inventor, Horace Smith, is right when he said, *"Inconsistency is the only thing in which men are consistent."*

Being consistent in what we do, and being persistent in taking actions can help us to achieve the results we want to see in our lives. In fact, I would prefer a person who is consistent over time, than a person who is on-fire for only a short time. Consistency can take a person far in life. Think about it: what if you are consistent in learning new things every day? What if you are consistent in training your body and trying to be healthy? What if you are consistent in trying to be a good parent? What difference will it make? In one year, you can be wiser than any of your other friends. In six months, you can lose a lot of pounds and develop a healthy physique. In one month, you can be closer to your child if and only if you are consistent in your approach to them. That's the power of consistency.

In this chapter, we will explore this topic in greater depth. I personally believe that taking steady steps towards your goal is the key to success and developing the habit of consistency is crucial to your life's work. Thus, you need to get this right. We will discuss the aspects of our lives that demand consistency. And lastly, we will answer the question: *"How do we become consistent?"*

The Millionaire That No One Knows!

The story of Anne Scheiber is one of the best illustrations of the power of consistency. She was a millionaire, but no one knew about it. The people who knew her thought she was just an old lady without any superior quality. To them, she was just any other old lady – nothing more, nothing less. However, at the time of her death, she left nearly all her estate to Yeshiva University amounting to $22 million! How did she do it? How she was able to amass so much wealth without any of her friends knowing? The answer – extraordinary commitment to consistency.

Anne Scheiber died in January 1995 at the age of 101 years old. She lived in a small apartment in the city of Manhattan with a rent of four hundred dollars a month. Most of her monthly income came from Social Security and a small monthly pension. Anne started receiving this sum of money in 1943 when she retired as an auditor of the Internal Revenue Service. And since then, she lived as a model of thrift. Benjamin Clark, who knew her personally said, *"She was treated very shabbily. She really had to fend for herself in every way. It was really quite a struggle."*

So, how did she do it? How was she able to accumulate $22 million within 50 years? By the time, Anne retired from IRS, she had already saved $5,000. She opted to invest in stocks and by 1950 she had enough profit to purchase shares of Schering-Plough Corporation – 1,000 shares to be exact. Anne held on to that stock and just let its value build overtime.

By the time of her death, her shares in that company had increased up to 128,000 with a value of $7.5 million. By applying the principle of consistency in her life, she became one of the richest ladies in Manhattan.

As consistency is important in the principle of building wealth, it is also more essential in the arena of success in life. Consistency demands we continue the pursuit despite what we feel or what we are going through. Just like Anne Scheiber. For sure, there were times during those 50 years that the value of her investments dropped. But instead of pulling out, she kept at it and stayed consistent and added more shares to her portfolio. The dividends that she was received she reinvested. Indeed, she understood the importance of consistency and thus she was able to accumulate that sum of money. The same is true when it comes to our lives.

The Importance of Consistency

Aldous Huxley, a prominent English Writer, insightfully said, *"Consistency is contrary to nature, contrary to life. The only completely consistent people are dead."* Being consistent in every aspect of your life is indeed important. It holds the key to the success of most of our endeavors. Most significant endeavors did not happen overnight. The success of famous people like Bill Gates, Steve Jobs and Mark Zuckerberg is not a product of a one-week effort. No, my friend, it doesn't happen that way. Every achievement and accomplishment is a result of taking steady and consistent actions daily. Indeed, there is no other way. Here are five things that describe the importance of consistency:

1. Consistency Improves your Skills

There were two neophyte computer programmers who started working for a company. Both had exceptional skills when it came to coding and using different programming language. In fact, both had honors upon graduating from university and despite their lack of actual work experience, their employers agreed they had the potential to become great in their field. However, they were completely different in the way they approached tasks given to them. The first programmer had a sense of urgency to work on the task immediately and submit it before time, while the second programmer was an easy-go-lucky guy who only worked on the task from time to time, yet still submitted it on time.

After several years, both learned a lot in their respective jobs and decided to apply to other companies. Ten years passed and the first programmer became the president of his own company while the second programmer was a senior IT personnel in the firm of his colleague. What was the difference? There was no significant deviation in what they did over the years, except during the night. You see, the first programmer decided to consistently learn new skills for two hours every night while the second programmer decided to consistently watch TV every night. Their two-hour habits performed consistently night after night made all the difference. Leadership expert, John Maxwell, said, *"Small disciplines repeated with consistency every day lead to great achievements gained slowly over time."*

If you want to improve a certain skill, then you need to be consistent in honing it. If you want to increase your wisdom in your expertise, then you need to be consistent in learning more about it. Let's face it, without consistency, there is no improvement. We can put ourselves into a strict regimen of training, but if we do not do it continually, then we cannot expect to see significant results in what we are trying to do. A writer who doesn't write will not get better at writing. A player who doesn't play will not get better at his game. Be consistent in practicing your craft, in executing your plans, and in improving your skills, and I guarantee you will see a significant difference in your performance over time.

2. Consistency Eliminates Mediocrity

If being consistent can improve your skills dramatically, then consistency will produce excellence which in turn eliminates mediocrity in our lives. Mediocrity is an enemy of success. If there is one thing that is more dangerous than non-performance, it is delivering an average output in the things that we do. Robert Green Ingersoll once said, *"In the Republic of Mediocrity, genius is dangerous."* Let's face it, in most of our circles, being average is the norm. Try to shoot for excellence and people will come in droves to shoot at you. People who challenge the status quo are not always liked, but they are the same people who can inspire excellence within the hearts of those willing to respond.

Being consistent will eliminate mediocrity by setting a new norm. When people are constantly being exposed to greatness, a new desire is created in their hearts and this desire asks, *"What if I can do that too?"*, *"What if I can achieve what he has achieved?"*, *"What if I also have the potential to accomplish great things?"* And the moment we start to ask ourselves those questions, this will begin the process of eliminating mediocrity in our lives. It doesn't matter if you're not good at first, if you have the capability to take consistent actions, then you can be successful. Michael Jordan said, *"I've missed more than 9,000 shots in my career."* Yet he is still one of the greatest men to play the ball. The secret of how he eliminated his mediocrity? It is consistency in the face of disappointment.

3. Consistency Develops your Character

Consistency can produce tremendous fruits of success in your life. However, as you already know, being consistent is also one of the most difficult tasks that an individual might try to accomplish. It is contrary to our nature. Let's face it, if we have a choice to stop doing something that gives us an uncomfortable feeling, most of the time we choose to stop, despite our knowledge that that particular activity can help us to grow and mature as a person. That is why I say that doing your best to be consistent in what you do can help you to develop your character.

Think about it. By striving hard to be consistent, you are

developing patience in yourself and with other people. You realize that no great thing comes easy. Some things can only be obtained by stubbornly refusing to stop in the pursuit of them.

John Maxwell quipped, *"Most people never realize how close they are to achieving things, because they give up too soon."* Indeed, if we are patient enough to wait and to continuously work hard, success will be inevitable.

Another aspect of our character that is being developed by being consistent is perseverance. One of the most saddening phenomena the Millennial generation is facing is their propensity to quit. In fact, the Bureau of Labor Statistics released data in 2015 showing three million Americans quit their job; the highest number since 2006. This is quite alarming because the research infers that these people, especially the Millennials, are prone to quitting.

As football player and coach, Vince Lombardi said, *"Once you learn to quit it becomes a habit."* Perseverance is slowly being out dated and one way to bring it back is to establish consistency in what we value, what we do, and what we are trying to accomplish.

4. Consistency Makes Things Easier

Being consistency is hard, but once you get the hang of it, the things that you are doing will become easy. We all know the principle of the learning curve. This principle simply says that the more one does something, the better they get at it. For instance, developing the habit to jog in the morning is hard. First, the idea of waking up earlier than the usual just to do exercise is repulsive for some people. Second, our body resists the additional burden that it has to endure by running a couple of miles. Therefore, starting the habit of jogging is hard.

However, the longer you keep at it, the easier it becomes for you. As you develop the habit of running every morning, you receive rewards in the form of self-fulfillment and increased self-esteem. These rewards will make the exercise easier.

Start doing something even if it is difficult at first. If you know in your heart that an activity can help you to grow and develop an important aspect in your life, then begin by taking small steps in doing it. Remember, you may not feel good just by doing something. However, as author Ernest Newman said, *"The great composer does not set to work because he is inspired, but becomes inspired because he is working. Beethoven, Wagner, Mozart, and Bach all settled down, day after day, to the job at hand. They didn't waste time waiting for inspiration."* The same should be true for you.

When we consistently devote ourselves to doing specific tasks, the more we cultivate a desire to do more of that thing. And here's the good news: as you are consistent, the more you learn and improve your skills. The more you learn and improve your skills, the easier the task will be. Again, consistency is the key. Tom Seaver said it more beautifully: *"In baseball, my theory is to strive for consistency, not to worry about the numbers. If you dwell on the statistics you get short-sighted, if you aim for consistency, the numbers will be there at the end."*

5. Consistency Increases Your Chances to Succeed

Success is not a sprint; it has and will always be a marathon. And you know who will be successful at the end? Those individuals who have the tenacity to run the miles of the journey ahead and look forward with enthusiasm to their desired destination. Is it easy? Of course, not. But these persons know that consistency has always been the key in winning this ultimate marathon of life. In fact, Frank Shorter, an American athlete, gave this advice for aspiring runners:

> *"For the novice runner, I'd say to give yourself at least two months of consistently running several times a week at a conversational pace before deciding whether you want to stick with it. Consistency is the most important aspect of training at this point."*

In any aspect of life, high achievers know that consistency plays a crucial part in achieving success. I will boldly say that without consistency, success is impossible. James Meston asserted, *"Success has a price tag on it, and the tag reads: courage, determination, discipline, risk taking, perseverance, and consistency – doing the right things for the right reasons and not just when we feel like it."* To accomplish small things, then exert effort occasionally, but to accomplish great things, then exert effort consistently.

When you steadily work on your skills, you will get better at them. The more you get better at what you do, the more you will become excel. When your excellence in skills is combined with the depth of your character, then success will be significantly closer to you. Indeed, consistency takes people to a lot of places!

Areas of Consistency

Now that we know the importance of being consistent in different aspects of our lives, now it is time to pinpoint the exact areas of our personal lives that need to be embedded with the consistency principle. Though I believe that it is crucial to develop this philosophy in your life, it is also equally important to determine the different areas of our lives that we need to change.

For instance, Tony Robbins said, *"Life is nothing but a mirror of your consistent thoughts."* Therefore, if you are thinking about negativities, then being consistent in doing that will do you more harm than good. If you are pursuing a goal which is not in accordance to your vision in life, then being consistent in that pursuit will just get you to fail faster. Consistency is important, but determining the proper sections of our lives where we need to be consistent is also important. Here are the areas where you must develop consistency.

1. Our Actions

Ideas and thoughts will be useless unless they are expressed in the physical realm through our actions. And most of the time, our bodies can't keep up with what our mind is currently thinking about. As our mind runs through every scenario and possibilities that can happen during execution, we can be overwhelmed with all the information we have, which in turn can result in *"paralysis by analysis."* This means we cannot decide to take action because we can't decide the course of action to take due to the vast information being presented to us. However, success in the physical realm can only be won through consistent actions, and not by just consistent thinking.

Closely related to the idea of consistent actions are habits. Habits are things we repeatedly do whether we are aware of them or not. To create a beneficial pattern that can help you in the long run, you need to take responsibility for your habits. Take note of what you consistently do and assess if that activity is helping or hampering your success. When it comes to habits, it is useful to note the advice of author Brian Tracy: *"Your subconscious mind makes all your words and actions fit a pattern consistent with your self-concept and your innermost beliefs about yourself."*

2. Our Self-Talk

In the previous chapters, I highlighted the importance of self-talk or the inner dialogue that happens to us every day. I also discussed the importance of taking responsibility for your self-talk and making it more positive to aid in life transformation. However, there is a recurring problem that we need to deal with repeatedly. It's our tendency to go back to saying negative things about ourselves. Let's face it, for someone who has low self-esteem, low self-confidence, and an inadequate view of himself, talking positively in a consistent manner is difficult. Yet, as Edmond Mbiaka commented, *"Consistent positive self-talk is unquestionably one of the greatest gifts to one's subconscious mind."*

So, how can a person be consistent in his inner dialogue? I believe simple tweaks and easy exercises can do the trick. By setting up a few reminders each day in the form of a phone alarm you can remember that, *"Hey, I was about to talk to myself more positively, right?"* then, respond immediately. You can also develop the habit of bringing a small mirror and talking to your reflection throughout the day. Or you can simply bring a small pack of cards with written positive assertions and sentences to take with you every day. Whatever it is that fits your style, do it. Just be consistent in speaking positively about yourself. Remember what entrepreneur and author, Robert Kiyosaki, said, *"It's not what you say out of your mouth that determines your life, it's what you whisper to yourself that has the most power."*

3. Our Personal Growth

Jim Rohn once said, *"If you want to reach your goals and fulfill your potential, you need to become intentional about your personal growth."* Yet, the exact opposite is what most individuals are doing. They put the idea of personal growth on the back burner in life. They are too busy with so many other things that spending a couple of hours to grow their knowledge and wisdom seems burdensome. Besides, what more do they need to learn? Let's face it, most of us love the idea of success but hate

the idea of the work necessary to achieve it –committing to your personal growth is one way to do it. We are like a child who makes it a habit to watch the television day and night and then wonders why she does not receive any medals or trophies.

My friend, you need to be consistent in pursuing personal growth because it's the only road that can bring you to lasting success. Be consistent in learning something new every day. I once read an apt illustration of a day in which you didn't learn anything new. Try to do it. If you didn't learn anything for the day, then get a piece of napkin and a matchbox. Light up the piece of napkin and watch as it burns and turns into heaps of ashes. Well, that is what happens when you don't learn something new. Your day will be wasted. If you are not growing, then you are not moving towards success. Heed the words of leadership speaker, Robin Sharma: *"The swiftest way to triple your success is to double your investment in personal development."*

4. Our Goals

I have already highlighted the idea of successful goal setting and goal getting. However, there is one area we still haven't covered. What if the goals you have set are too hard and you can't seem to get anywhere near them. Will you change the goals? Or do you have to stay consistent with achieving them? Let me answer those questions considering the assumption that you have carefully crafted your goal using the S-M-A-R-T method. In this method, your goal is indeed *"attainable."* The problem here is not really the goal but the way you approach it and the actions you take in getting it.

If you have ever tried to set a goal and done your best to achieve it, then you know that there are times when plans do not happen as expected. In times like this, we are tempted to change the goals that we have set for ourselves. We think that maybe we have set the bar too high and can't really do it. However, as motivational speaker Zig Ziglar said, *"As you head toward your goals, be prepared to make some slight adjustments to your course. You don't change your decision to go – you do change the direction to get there."* You need to be more flexible in your methods of execution, if something did not work after a couple of tries, then try something new. Don't be afraid to experiment, because in life, the people who learn the most are those who have been exposed several times to their mistakes and failures.

Be consistent in your goals. If you have spent ample time considering everything before writing it down, then it should be the right goal for you. Encountering setbacks are natural; in fact, I would be bold enough to say that if you are not experiencing major setbacks in the process of getting your goals, then you are not making significant advancements. So, do not be afraid to come across a couple of walls in the process of achieving your goals. Just change your method; either you break through the wall or you get a ladder to climb over it. Don't be afraid of change. John Maxwell asserted, *"Reaching new goals and moving to a higher level of performance always require change, and change feels awkward. But take comfort in the knowledge that if a change doesn't feel uncomfortable, then it's probably not really a change."*

Building Consistency 101

At this point, you already have an idea of the crucial role that consistency plays in our pursuit of success. It is indispensable because consistency has been and will always be a key to significant achievements in your life. If you would like to continually climb the ladder of success and reach new heights in the different aspects of your life, then you cannot ignore consistency.

The question now is this: *How can I be consistent?* Yes, consistency is difficult because it is against our nature. We are living in the age of instant gratification and waiting for a result while consistently working in your discipline is not really appealing. However, though it might be difficult, it is not impossible. You can always take the necessary steps needed to build your own *"Consistency Manifesto"*. If you desire to develop the quality of consistency, then do the following:

1. Develop a System

Consistency is built on the idea of repetition. If you can repeat a useful activity that you do today and do it again tomorrow, the next week, and the next month, then you can be consistent. Building a system will help you to accomplish just that. What is a system? Leadership expert John Maxwell defined system as follows:

"A process for predictably achieving a goal based on specific, orderly, repeatable principles and practices."

Let us try to elaborate on each individual point.

- *Predictable* – A system must provide a predictable pattern that can give you a feel of what will happen in the days to come. For instance, you can set up a system of how you would improve your knowledge by reading a book a month. This will give you the ability to predict that within a year, you will be able to read 12 books.
- *Specific* – A system must include specific functions that you can easily identify. Take for example the different systems inside the human body. All parts of the system have a name and a function. When you experience any irregularities within your body, the doctors can pin point the exact problem by looking at the specific parts and their function. That's how a system works.
- *Orderly* – You can't call a system a *"system"* if there is no order. If there are no defined rules and regulations, then your system will be reduced to a list of useful tips and advice, but not really a complete set of activities that aim to reach a common goal. To add order to your system, define the step-by-step process that must happen.
- *Repeatable* – The system you must create must have the quality of repeatability. It doesn't matter if the tasks and functions you added in the system are useful, but if you can't repeat the process your system will fail. For instance, talking with a mentor is ideal to develop wisdom. However, if your system demands that you talk to a mentor every day, then it would be impossible for you to repeat it as expected.
- *Principles and practices* – A good system includes both. You can't live on principles alone, but you can't thrive with only

practices either. Both are needed to have a successful system. The principles act as the guide, while the practices are the vehicle that can get you to your destination.

Practicing consistency will be greatly enhanced if you put strong systems in place. By having a system, you can carefully identify the different tasks to complete, as well as the capability to diagnose if there is anything wrong in the process you are taking to achieve your goals. Systems are a great tool in improving consistency.

As Michael Gerber, the author of E-Myth, said, *"Systems permit ordinary people to achieve extraordinary results predictably. However, without a system, even extraordinary people find it difficult to predictably achieve even ordinary results."*

2. Use the Power of Scheduling

In order to take advantage of the benefits of consistency, then you must also utilize the power of scheduling. This is simple. All you have to do is to use a calendar and list down the different dates and time you intend to do an activity. For instance, if you want to be consistent in growing yourself by reading a book, then you can set a time of the day, five o'clock in the afternoon as an example, to do that task. By committing to the schedule, you have set, you are enabling yourself to predictably accomplish the set tasks.

Without scheduling, then you are bound to fail in doing your tasks consistently. Assume that in the example above, instead of writing every afternoon at five o'clock, you state it in this way: *"I will read the book every day."* Now, my friend, by doing this, you have included the whole 24 hours in your schedule. However, when it comes to scheduling, it's better to be specific. If there is no specified time for execution, then it is unlikely be executed, thus defeating the very purpose of consistency.

3. Find Regular Time for Breaks

Now, you might be asking, *"What's the principle of taking a break do in the discussion of consistency?"* Well, I can tell you that it has a lot to do when it comes to consistency. Let me elaborate. The *Pomodoro Technique,* developed by Francesco

Cirillo in the 1980s, is one of the most useful techniques that I have used when it comes to writing. For a writer like me, being consistent in writing a lot of content is a must. However, there is always a challenge to maintain focus, concentrate on what I must do, and my overall productivity in doing my writing tasks.

So, what did I do to address it? I used the *Pomodoro Technique* of focused writing within 25 minutes, then taking short breaks for about three to five minutes, before continuing writing for another 25 minutes.

Using this technique enabled me to bring up my productivity to a higher notch. I increased my focus and my concentration, and I'm writing more words every day. Now, if you look closely, you'll notice that even this productivity technique banks on breaks. It encourages individuals to take shorter breaks of three to five minutes in four sets of 25 minutes, then a longer break of 30 minutes after the first four sets. It seems an irony that taking a break can make you more consistent and productive, but that is the truth. In fact, recent studies back this up. In a study of University of Illinois at Urbana-Champaign, researchers concluded that brief diversions from the task at hand vastly improve the focus of a person.

It's difficult to run on fumes. If you want to stay longer and more productive at what you do, then you need to take regular breaks too. It serves as a fuel and can give us a much needed boost to continue performing at high levels. Stand up, take a short walk, stretch your body, whatever it is, make it a point to have regular breaks. Even the most successful people need time to unwind and renew their strength. So, don't be too hard on yourself when you are taking a break.

4. Find Accountability Partners

Another great way to improve your consistency is to find people who will keep you accountable in what you are trying to accomplish. Left on our own, we can wander and not follow through on our plans. But when we have other people checking our progress and constantly challenging us about our commitment to consistency, then we are being forced to level up. In Proverbs

27:17 of the Bible it says: *"As iron sharpens iron, so a friend sharpens a friend."* Both you and your friends can benefit from the power of accountability by holding each other responsible for keeping promises to follow through on.

High achievers like Michael Jordan, Mike Tyson, Arnold Schwarzenegger, and Georges St-Pierre are successful. However, these individuals have something in common that was instrumental for them to achieve their level of success.

All of them have their own accountability partners, in the form of a coach, trainer or business partner, where they are responsible to report their progress and anything related to what they want to accomplish. Indeed, having an accountability partner can give you a boost in succeeding and in developing consistency in your life.

5. Discipline Yourself

The last of the steps in develop consistency is to cultivate self-discipline. Everything that we have discussed so far when it comes to consistency – in fact, the whole book – will be all for naught if you are unsuccessful in disciplining yourself. Setting up a stable system with all the necessary functions will be useless if you cannot discipline yourself to follow through. Having a detailed schedule is meaningless if you are not doing what you are supposed to be doing at the specified time. Taking breaks is pointless if you don't have anything to do but take a break. And finding an accountability partner is worthless if you can't keep your word by working on your goals. You see, all these tips are highly dependent on the way you discipline yourself.

Let's face it, without discipline, consistency is impossible. However, as American President Theodore Roosevelt once said, *"With self-discipline, most anything is possible."* There are things that are reserved only for individuals who take on the challenge of disciplining themselves in doing what they need to do. Of all the advice, I give you when it comes to cultivating your consistency, I believe that self-discipline is the hardest because it strikes at the heart of our being.

We resist anything that makes us uncomfortable, we avoid those things that push us to exert extra effort, and we hate committing ourselves to a set of rules and regulations. Yet, if you truly want to develop consistency, then you need to be disciplined.

Here's President Theodore Roosevelt's complete quote that I hope will encourage you to challenge yourself and embrace self-discipline:

"The one quality which sets one man apart from another – the key which lifts one to every aspiration while others are caught up in the mire of mediocrity – is not talent, formal education, nor intellectual brightness – it is self-discipline.

With self-discipline, most anything is possible. Without it, even the simplest goal can seem like an impossible dream."

Consistently Consistent

"You don't buy consistency, you learn to be decisively consistent by avoiding procrastination and making excuses" – Chindah Chindah

If you want to achieve more of your goals, if you want to accomplish great things, if you want to grow yourself and make a significant impact on the lives of others, then you can't ignore the principle of consistency.

Remember, you have the potential to make all your dreams come true, but that is entirely dependent on what you will consistently do to do it. If you are consistently inconsistent, then you won't be able to reach your destination, people will not respect you and won't believe your word. However, if you embrace consistency, then people will see your integrity and it will only be a matter of time before you achieve your highest goals in life. So be consistently consistent!

Discussion Questions and Reflections:

This portion of each chapter aims to establish the concepts and principles that you have learned so far. Try to carefully consider each question and answer it with a complete reflection of how it applies to your life. I would also implore you to take notes and even share what you have learned with others to initiate healthy discussion.

1. Do you believe consistency is important for a person? Can you think of a moment where consistency has been a crucial aspect of your success or failure? Why do you think that being consistent is an essential element of accomplishment? Can you also give other benefits or advantages of being consistent?

_____

_____

2. On a scale of 1 to 10, 10 being the highest and 1 the lowest, rate yourself in terms of your overall consistency. Based on your answer, what do you think is the reason for your level of consistency? What areas of your life or aspects of your personality do you need to be more consistent? What do you think are the significant changes that can happen if you are consistent in that aspect?

_____

_____

3. Based on your own experience, what is the importance of self-discipline in different areas of your life? Do you believe that being self-disciplined can get you closer to your goals faster? Why? In what area of your life do you need to be more disciplined? What actions will you take to improve your discipline in that area?

_____

_____

_____

EXPECTATION ≠ REALITY

CHAPTER 6

*"Life is 10% what happens to you
and 90% how you react to it."*

– Charles Swindoll

The principle of personal development and self-improvement can bring tremendous motivation for those people who embrace the need for it. The idea of getting better as a person and making greater impact on the lives of other people can give an individual the needed inspiration to accomplish significant endeavors. The possibilities are endless and the potential are limitless. We all want that. We all want to be under the euphoria that we are part of something bigger than ourselves. And these emotions of excitement can help us get started in the process. As Mark Twain asserted, *"The secret of getting ahead is getting started."*

''The greatest risk you will ever take is the risk of staying in your comfort zone while your dreams, talents, purpose and life mission is unfulfilled'' – Chindah Chindah

Yes, the idea of getting started can set our souls on fire. However, what if the reality that we need to face is totally different from all our expectations? What if the clear road that we dream of is an unpaved path full of rocks and briers? What if the road to success is on the collision path with the road to failure? What should we do? How should we react?

What are we to do when expectation is nothing like the reality that we are about to face? Dr. Steve Maraboli paints this particular scenario without sugar coating: *"Expectation feeds frustration. It is an unhealthy attachment to people, things, and outcomes we wish we could control; but don't."*

If that is true, then does it mean that we should stop building expectations within our minds? Does it mean that we should resist the urge to anticipate the results that we want from life? I believe the answer is "no." Indeed, in life, most of the time the reality of our lives is entirely different from what we expect. However, that doesn't mean we need to stop expecting. What we need to do is to create an expectation that closely mirrors reality. That is what this chapter is all about.

The goal of this chapter is to help you to face the realities of committing yourself to personal development. I will also discuss with you the most common response when people are faced with the *"Expectation vs. Reality"* syndrome. After that, you will learn the process of re-evaluation, which is one of the most important skills you can acquire if you are to be successful in improving yourself. And lastly, we will try to identify the different areas that need to be adjusted in our lives. The road to success is not a straight and brightly lit path. It is a dark alley where a lot of uncertainties lurk. However, you don't have to worry because a flashlight will be given to you. The principles you learn in this chapter can be your spare batteries.

Dreams. Troubles. Redemption.

The story of Joseph the Dreamer in the Bible is one of those stories that show how the need to adapt and adjust can help you to overcome obstacles in your life. You can find the whole story of his life in Genesis 37, but let me share with you a summary of what happened to him. Joseph was the favorite son of his father, Israel, and because of this, all his brothers hated him. In addition to this, Joseph also had dreams that symbolized how his brothers and his parents would bow down to him in respect. That made him hated by his brothers.

I can imagine Joseph having a great plan for his life. He was young and energetic and he had the full support of his father. But one day, his brothers conspired to kill him, yet in the end they just sold him as a slave to the caravans who were going to Egypt. Imagine the dismay that Joseph felt during that time. He had been sold out by his own brothers and was forced to work as a slave in Egypt. His reality was totally different from his expectations, but he did not let it stop him. Because of Joseph's excellent administrative skills, he immediately gained the trust of his master which made him the "*household manager.*"

However, the good times didn't last for long. His master's wife took special notice of Joseph's handsomeness and sought to commit adultery with him. In a negative chain of events, Joseph was accused of attempting to rape his master's wife and landed in prison.

Again, the expectations of Joseph were entirely altered by the reality that beset him. But then again, he did what he could to adjust his situation. Even in prison, Joseph did the best that he could and in time, he helped run the entire prison. A couple of significant things happened, but in the end, Joseph became successful until he was second-in-command to the king of Egypt.

It's easy to be consumed by disappointments when things don't happen as planned. Joseph encountered a lot of disappointing events in his life, but instead of wallowing in self-pity, he recovered from the pain and trouble, and did what he could to adjust to the situation. In the arena of self-improvement, the same thing can happen in your life. The only question is: will you be like Joseph and step back from disappointment and adapt to the situation to make it better for you? As legendary coach John Wooden said, "*Things turn out best for those who make the best of the way things turn out.*"

The Realities of Personal Development

While improving yourself, there are moments when significant changes take place that will considerably affect the realities you have to face. You can't expect the road to success to be smooth sailing because it is not. There are troubles waiting for you along the way. There are problems #you need to solve. However, this should not intimidate or discourage you because as Paul Harvey once said, "*You can always tell when you are on the road to success: it's uphill all the way.*"

So, if trials are inevitable, what you can do right now is to identify the negative possibilities that can happen and prepare for it accordingly.

1. The Initial Motivation Wanes

Have you ever experienced going to a seminar where you heard a great motivational speaker who inspired you with his speech? You laughed, you related to what he was saying, and your heart was touched by the message he delivered. In fact, you couldn't contain the inspiration and excitement you experienced that you couldn't wait to go home and apply everything that you had learned. However, after a few days you just don't feel the same level of motivation anymore. And before you know it, you are back to the old you, thinking the same thoughts, talking in the same way, and doing the same actions. Nothing has changed.

This is a common phenomenon for most people. Personal development is indeed an inspiring goal to achieve. However, despite its tremendous benefits to a person, people still have a way of resigning from the initial motivations they received. We are so quick to go back to our old habits and to our old selves. And you need to be prepared for that. At this moment, let it be clear to you that initial motivation doesn't last for too long.

So, if you want to continue in your personal development, then you need to anchor your new habits to a force that is stronger than the initial motivation. E.M. Gray supports the argument by saying, *"The successful person has the habit of doing the things that failures don't like to do."*

The successful person doesn't like doing them either, but his dislike is subordinated to the strength of his purpose. Author and journalist George Lorimer once said, *"You've got to get up every morning with determination if you're going to bed with satisfaction."*

2. Force Majeure Happens

Force Majeure is a French term that literally means *"greater force."* It pertains to those things that you can't control but have the potential to alter your life. As I have said earlier, the road to success is a dark alley with lots of stones and briers that can hurt you. In the pursuit of what you want to accomplish, unexpected things are bound to happen and sometimes, these things are not good.

Maybe you are trying your best to improve your knowledge by reading books, but there is an unexpected leak in your roof that dampens all your books. Or maybe you are meeting a mentor, but then your mentor decides to move to another location which made it virtually impossible for you to meet him/her regularly. Or perhaps you are trying to save money but a disease has struck your child so you don't have a choice but to spend the money that you have saved.

Force Majeure is a part of life. And indeed, it can change the way we see and do things. But since we can't escape it, then we just need to be ready for it. How? By taking responsibility for our attitudes. People have the tendency to gripe and blame other people when bad things happen. However, by realizing that in spite of some random circumstances that we can do nothing about, we still have complete control over our emotions, then we can rise above the circumstances of our lives.

Stephen Covey in his classic book, *"The 7 Habits of Highly Effective People"* discusses the habit of proactivity. In this habit is the realization that we have two circles in our lives when it comes to the things that we worry about. The average person's first circle is the *"Circle of Concern."* These are the things that you think about but you can do nothing about such as politics, the weather, and the actions of people around you. You are concerned about these things, but you can't directly control them. Inside the *"Circle of Concern"* is a smaller circle called the *"Circle of Influence".* This represents those things that we have total control over like our emotions, our response and the breakfast that we want to eat tomorrow.

Now, here's the clincher, most people focus on their Circle of Concern and give little attention to their Circle of Influence. It means that most of us are so stressed about what is happening in politics, freaking out about the weather tomorrow, and constantly worrying about what other people think about us. However, if you look closely, you can really do nothing about these things, right? These things are real problems, but like *Force Majeure,* an individual does not have power over them. My suggestion is to learn to live with things inside your Circle of Concern while at the same time take care of things inside your Circle of Influence. And as Stephen Covey said himself, *"The main thing is to keep the main thing the main thing."*

3. You Might be Overwhelmed

The task of self-improvement is indeed an inspiring goal. The idea of personal development can open our mind to the unlimited potential that is lying dormant in each one of us. And when we realize the things that we can do once we embrace the process of personal development, we get excited. However, without proper control over your emotions, you can easily get overwhelmed by the daunting tasks ahead. Changing your old habits of years is difficult enough, but you need to also add new habits to your artillery. Old mindsets pose the greatest challenge. It's hard to renew our thinking, refine our focus and overhaul our perspective. Indeed, there will be times where you will fail in what you are trying to do.

I believe that is also one of the reasons why people settle for their old lives than do the hard work of tearing down the outdated thought-patterns and build new ones. As Charles Brower once said, *"Most people are more comfortable with old problems than with new solutions."* Another reason for quitting personal development is by seeing the whole perspective of what you want to accomplish. The process of self-improvement is painfully slow in the beginning so a lot of individuals stop. I'm not saying these things to discourage you, I'm saying these things to help you prepare better for what lies ahead.

My advice for you is to just get started. Zig Ziglar asserted, *"Do not try to overcome all the obstacles before you even begin."* There will be problems alright, but you don't need to solve those things all at once and thus the axiom: *we will cross that bridge when we come to it.* These are painful realities of aiming for personal development, but before you throw in the towel, let the following words from leadership expert John Maxwell inspire you:

"Motivation is not going to strike you like lightning. And motivation is not something someone else can bestow or force on you. The whole idea of motivation is a trap. Forget motivation. Just do it.

"Do it without motivation and then guess what? After you start doing the thing, that's when motivation comes and makes it easy for you to keep on doing it."

The RE's

In its most basic sense, personal development is built on the idea that something must be built. And in this building process, some strongholds must be demolished while new structures must be constructed. Yet, as with any construction project, there are different circumstances that might affect the whole venture. The erection of the building doesn't stop with the architecture finishing the blue print. In fact, it just signifies the beginning. The true work begins when builders starts the project. And again, during this time, various things might come up that might speed up or delay the construction. Individuals have different reactions to this change. Here are some of them:

1. Resent

When confronted with a possible delay in achieving a goal, some people become resentful. They resent themselves for bothering to start the process, or they resent other people and blame them for the delay. However, as we have noted earlier, we cannot control our circumstances, because there will always be an *"unknown"* factor that must be considered. Harboring resentment is a sign of immaturity and being unprepared to deal with the idea of change. Personal development is not easy and if you get angry about changes with your plans, then personal development is not for you.

2. Regret

Sometimes when people fail in achieving their goals, they feel a profound sense of regret. However, the regret that they feel is not because they failed but because of the reason they started in the first place. Their inner dialogue goes something like this, *"I knew it. I should have not done this in the first place. Who am I? I'm too ambitious. I dream too big! I don't deserve success. I should just stay in my current situation."* So, they regret trying. However, if they only know that achieving success is hard then they would be better prepared to handle disappointments.

There must not be regret in trying. Mark Twain asserted, *"Twenty years from now you will be more disappointed by the things you didn't do than by the ones you did do."* I believe that the greatest regret a person can experience is being an old man, lying on the bed and thinking to himself, *"What if I tried? I could have achieved my dreams. I would have unleashed my potential. I would have created a significant impact."*

Don't let this be you. Try new things, especially inside the arena of personal development. If you fail, then you fail. Learn from it, and then move on.

3. Resist

There are people who will commit a mistake in the process of developing themselves, yet upon confronting their shortcomings, they resist change and adjustment. Instead of learning from what they did wrong, they stubbornly refuse to acknowledge the things they did wrong and repeatedly commit the same mistake repeatedly. They believe in the saying, *"You can't teach new tricks to old dogs."* So, they hold on to what they know and resist learning. Yet, in this process of being obstinate, they just get stuck where they fell.

Being persistent in your pursuit of success is highly recommended, yet you need to also have a discerning heart to know when to stop and think about the next course of actions you need to take. If your watch is not working, then bring it to the watchmaker and have it repaired, however, if after fixing the watch, it just returned to its old problem, then just get it lost. It's the same with our tactics and strategies; if something does not work, then try it again a couple of times, if still doesn't work, then consider strategizing again and coming up with a new solution. As author Robert Kiyosaki said, *"Don't waste a good mistake. Learn from it."*

To encourage you to build a healthy attitude in the face of failure and change, here is a piece from Portia Nelson called, *"Autobiography in Five Short Chapters"*:

Chapter 1:

I walk down the street. There is a deep hole in the sidewalk. I fall in. I am lost ... I am helpless. It isn't my fault. It takes me forever to find a way out.

Chapter 2:

I walk down the same street. There is a deep hole in the sidewalk. I pretend I don't see it. I fall in again. I can't believe I am in the same place but, it isn't my fault. It still takes a long time to get out.

Chapter 3:

I walk down the same street. There is a deep hole in the sidewalk. I see it is there. I still fall in ... it's a habit. My eyes are open. I know where I am. It is my fault. I get out immediately.

Chapter 4:

I walk down the same street. There is a deep hole in the sidewalk. I walk around it.

Chapter 5:

I walk down another street.

Don't resist it. If there's a need to change in your method of achieving success, then do it. Be stubborn in getting your goals, but be flexible in your methods of doing it. Learn from your mistakes and try to do it a little better. Sometimes working harder and faster is not the answer, but being a little wiser is.

4. Return

Perhaps, the saddest response of people who have started their personal development journey is choosing to return to old habits. Because they couldn't achieve a certain level of accomplishment, they decide that they are **not** good enough and return to how they lived before. What's troubling here is that all the time and effort that they had exerted goes to waste. All the hard work and determination that they poured out during their mission to better themselves was for naught. No, you should never return. You can rest, but don't attempt to return to the old you.

Returning to your old self is like spitting on all that you have tried to accomplish and calling it rubbish. Yes, trying to let go of your old self and exerting effort to let the new you emerge can be quite frightening. However, by leaving your old self – your old habits, old pattern of thoughts, and old perspective – you can take the step forward to discover what you are truly capable of achieving. Take a rest, but don't return. There is so much waiting for you on the other side of the dark alley of success.

5. Reevaluate

Now, this response is what high achievers do. When they hit a wall that seems to block them in going to their desired destination, they will try to break it by sheer force using the method that they have identified beforehand. If the wall still won't budge, then they will sit and quietly think about the reason they ended up there. Their inner dialogue goes something like this: *"How did I end up here? What did I do wrong? Is there any problem with my chosen method? Am I taking things faster than I should be?"* This is a process called *re-evaluation*.

Dan Miller asserted, *"Change, even if unwelcome, forces us to re-evaluate what our best options are. Those times of transitions are great opportunities to look for recurring patterns in your life and make adjustments to build on the good and reduce the bad."* People who choose to re-evaluate remove resentment because they know they have total control of how they feel. The circumstances they are in right now might not be ideal, but the situation won't change their feelings about achieving their goals. They also do away with regret, besides it's their choice why they are in this current situation. Instead of regret, they feel an uncommon feeling of excitement and thrill over what can happen. They certainly don't resist change and of course, returning to their old selves is not an option to them.

The principle of re-evaluation enables the person to consider carefully what happens in the past to pinpoint the exact cause of the problem. It also helps him to see the available courses of actions to take and what is the best path to take. And lastly, it gives him a positive perspective that this setback is proof he is indeed advancing.

It won't hurt you or the process of achieving your aim of personal development by taking a step back and seeing things from a wider perspective.

These five RE's might not capture all the possible responses people have in regards a change of plans. However, the aim of this section is to help you become aware that troubles are inevitable when you try to improve yourself, and be aware of the different responses you can feel when confronting change. I hope you will consistently choose what is right.

The Process of Re-evaluation

Yes, indeed, unforeseen circumstances might happen while improving yourself. And the best course of action to take is re-evaluating your situation and to determine the best options available to you. In the book *"The Art of War"* by Chinese military strategist Sun Tzu, he said, *"All warfare is based on deception. If your enemy is superior, evade him. If angry, irritate him. If equally matched, fight and if not: split and re-evaluate."* So how does this process of re-evaluation work? You can consider the following guidelines in doing your own re-evaluation:

1. Review Your Goals

Any realistic and useful re-evaluation process begins by going back to what you have planned before you even begin. Go back to your goals. Review the milestones that you have set. Remind yourself again of what you are trying to accomplish there. Any worthy goals and any significant endeavors do not happen overnight. It could take days, weeks, months or even years, thus constant review is of utmost importance. In fact, Les Brown quipped, *"Review your goals twice every day to be focused in achieving them."*

Remember your S-M-A-R-T goals that you set in the beginning. How do you specifically define the things that you want to accomplish? How can you measure the progress you are making? Is the goal truly attainable in your current state? Is it still relevant to your values and long term agenda in life? Is the time you have set still enough? Set aside a day to carefully revisit every aspect of your goals. If possible, try to remind yourself of the intangible things that caused you to set your goals. Remember your motivations. Think about the circumstances surrounding the day you started crafting your goal statement. Look deeper to answer the question: *"Why did I start doing this in the first place?"*

Now, if you are easily achieving your goals and you don't have anything to review today, then it could mean that you are setting yourself up for success. However, this kind of success could be shallow because it did not involve any hard work on your part.

I once read a quotation that said, *"If you haven't felt like quitting your dreams aren't big enough."* The problem is that little dreams produce impotent goals, and impotent goals lead us to a mediocre life. Olympic swimmer Michael Phelps shared that sentiment: *"I think goals should never be easy, they should force you to work, even if they are uncomfortable at the time."*

2. Measure Actual Results vs. Goals

After reviewing the goals that you have set in the beginning of your pursuit towards personal development, it is time to measure the results you have achieved. Now, two things might happen here. First, you can be discouraged by realizing you are too far from what you are aiming at. Second, you can be conceited and overconfident that you are easily getting your 'impotent' goals. Or you could choose a third response: celebrate how far you've got and be challenged by how much more you need to do.

If you have crafted your goal based on the S-M-A-R-T method, then this part is easy. You just compared your current numbers with the measurement that you have set in the beginning. For instance, if your goal was to lose 20lbs during the process of self-improvement, then just get a weighing scale and take note of your current weight. The difference is the gap that you still need to cover. However, the challenge here is the possibility of measuring intangibles. For example, if your goal is to influence 20 people, then how can you quantify it?

How can you say that you have indeed influenced 20 people? Is talking to them once enough measure to say that you have influenced their lives? Or do you measure it by seeing them taking some specific actions?

When it comes to your goal measurement, you need to be creative. And another thing to remember is to consider the Circle of Concern and the Circle of Influence. Don't set goals on things inside your Circle of Concern. It will be extremely difficult for you to achieve goals that are outside of your control. For instance, based on the examples above, setting a goal of influencing 20 people is complicated to measure and poses a challenge because you can't control the response of the other person. You might do all the things you know and can to influence him/her, but if they don't want to be influenced by you, then you can't do anything about that.

3. Adjust the Necessary Components

I strongly believe that goals must never be adjusted, except of course for extremely rare circumstances where you have no choice but to change it. With that said, I believe the process of re-evaluation will be complete once you come up with ideas and concepts about how you can break through the wall that is blocking your path right now. Will using a ladder help you? Is there a way around the wall that won't compromise your values and principles in life? Can you use a stronger force to demolish the wall? Or you are headed in the wrong way and that's why you have encountered the wall? These questions must be considered during the re-evaluation process. It is not enough to realize that you are stuck, what's important is to know what to do because you are stuck.

When you identify the different aspects of yourself that need adjustment, then it is time to get moving again. Overcome the barrier and move towards your desired destination. It doesn't matter how many times you do this. Re-evaluation is always a significant component of major endeavors. Now, if it is any comfort to you, do you know that an airplane is off course 99% of the time? However, despite this, it is amazing how the pilot can land the plane to its destination. The answer lies in the constant adjustment that the pilot does throughout the flight. When the plane gets off course, he does some minor adjustments. This process will continue until the pilot reaches the place where it wants to go.

People who are brave enough to tackle the idea of personal development in their lives and live according to its principle will inevitably need to deal with these kinds of problems. It doesn't matter whether you are the richest, the smartest, or the strongest man alive. When you set goals to improve yourself, you are likely to be off course most of the time. But this is not what matters most, because again, there are things that will be outside our Circle of Influence. What truly matters is our response to those setbacks that we are about to encounter in our journey to success. Life is a series of re-evaluation, it is a series of adjustments, and it is a series of correction. Don't be afraid to fail because failures are essential parts of success.

Adjustment Bureau

When it comes to exerting effort to improve yourself, there are certain aspects in your life that need to be adjusted frequently. When it comes to personal development, flexibility is always an important trait. If you can't adapt, you can't get to the top. If you can't adjust, you risk being last. That's the unspoken rule of self-improvement. Improvement is built on the foundation that to improve something, there is something that must be changed. Without change there can be no improvement or development.

Nobel Peace Prize recipient, John Boyd Orr, once said, "*Our civilization has evolved through the continuous adjustment of society to the stimulus of new knowledge."* Whenever there is updated information available to us, an adjustment must happen accordingly. In the arena of personal development, new information might pertain to new skills needed, methods that can give better results, or motivation that needed to be wane. These are the things that need to be adjusted as you go through the process of self-improvement.

1. Adjust Your Skills

The skill of a person is an important measurement of his level of capability. The things that you could achieve and the goals that you can accomplish are greatly dependent on the level of your skills. For instance, a graduate of medicine cannot perform a delicate heart surgery if he doesn't have the skills and mastery to do it.

Whenever someone is trying to achieve a target that is out of his league, there are only two things that can happen, and all is dependent on the adjustment that he will do on his skills. First, if he dedicates himself to acquiring and improving his skills, then he might hit the higher target. Second, if he stays at his level of expertise, then he will reap failure and won't achieve his goal.

Jim Rohn insightfully commented regarding the matter. He said, *"You must either modify your dreams or magnify your skills."* If you don't want to improve your skills, then you must be prepared to change your goals. And that is not in any way beneficial to self-improvement. So, how do you go about this? How can you make skills improvement a daily part of your life? Here are some suggestions:

a. Commit to lifelong learning

Commitment is another important, but often overlooked aspect of personal development. Most people think that they can improve themselves by just reading a book *from time to time* or attending a seminar once a year. However, that mindset is absolutely wrong. Personal development must be an everyday process and therefore, commitment to lifelong learning is a must.

Denis Waitley says it more beautifully: *"All of the top achievers I know are lifelong learners. Looking for new skills, insights, and ideas. If they're not learning, they're not growing and not moving toward excellence."*

b. Create a system to learn something new every day

The next step would be to flesh out your commitment to lifelong learning and this could be done by learning new things every day. There are different ways to do this. Some people make it a habit to read books. Others listen to podcasts or audio cd's. And still others use the habit of writing in a journal.

Whatever method that will work for you, then commit to doing it every day. Make it a habit. Don't let a day pass by without fleshing out your commitment to continual learning. Brian Herbert quipped, *"The capacity to learn is a gift. The ability to learn is a skill. The willingness to learn is a choice."*

c. Find ways to apply what you learn

Learning is not complete if there is no application of the acquired knowledge. Getting new information without a clear plan of application is like getting an electrical appliance without an electrical outlet to get power. Knowledge demands to be applied. If you are not applying what you learn, then you can't learn with integrity because all you have are dry facts.

Most people think that acquiring knowledge is all they ever need. However, when application is missing, all they have are ideals that they learned from someone. However, experiencing it personally is what takes your knowledge to experience and from experience to life lesson. Besides, skill is not just about what you know; skill is all about what you can do.

Adjusting your skills is a big step towards improving yourself. If you can just acquire one new skill and gain mastery over it every year, then think about what you can do and what you can accomplish after five years.

2. Adjust Your Method

All of us have a chosen way of doing things. All of us might be doing task, but the approach that we use to accomplish it will vary from person to person. Now, it is a known fact that some approaches are better than others. Who do you think will get the job done faster when it comes to cutting down a full-grown tree? Is it the one who is using a small knife or a person who is using a chainsaw? It's the same thing with who will be the person who can get faster to a certain destination; is it the one who took a straight path or the one who took the road with lots of turns and detours? We all know the answer to both questions.

Adjusting your method is all about choosing an approach to get your desired results faster. However, before we move forward, I believe that it is important to note that I'm not advocating here the use of shortcut methods that violate the timeless principles of life. I am not saying you should cheat to get your desired outcome or you pay for someone to do the task which you should be doing. What I'm saying here is there are different approaches to doing certain tasks, and to get to your goal faster, then you must choose the approach that can give you that result.

For instance, all of us know the timeless principle of sowing and reaping. It simply states that what you sow, you will reap. If you sow hard work, then you will reap success. If you sow laziness, then you will reap nothing but dust and ashes. Now, if you are a farmer, there is only one way to harvest agricultural produce from the land and that is by reaping. However, there are different approaches to this and each approach can give you different results. If you scatter the seeds without plowing the land first, then your results might be slower. But if you take the time to plow the land first to make it more conducive for plant growth, then there is a greater chance of getting your desired results.

That analogy is the same with personal development. Your chosen method will determine the result you get. Therefore, if you are not happy with the result you get, perhaps it is time to consider trying another method. Tony Robbins said it crisply, *"If you do what you've always done, you'll get what you've always gotten."* Now, the question here is, how will you know the right approach that you would use? Consider the following suggestions to get you started:

1. Ask questions

Asking yourself questions can help you discover a lot of things about yourself. *Are you happy with the results that you are getting? Do you feel comfortable with the approach that you are using? Is your method of execution in line with your areas of strength?* These are crucial questions. Remember this word – optimize. That should be your goal in every method that you use.

2. Look at Other People

There are a lot of things that you can learn by looking at other people and seeing how they do certain tasks. The idea of mimicking others when it comes to best practices is not a bad idea. In fact, if you take the time to look at how experts work, then you can gain valuable insights with regards to the best method of execution.

For instance, if you want to be a great public speaker, then you should watch and listen to how popular public speakers do their thing. I believe that you have your own voice and style. However, sometimes it will only surface once you have done the work of watching others doing it. In fact, if you listen to high achievers, you'll know that they always have someone to look up to.

3. Don't be afraid to experiment

One reason why we don't want to deviate from the traditional ways of doing things is because we don't want to fail. We don't want to come face to face with mistake and realize that we are wrong in trying something new. Yet, if you think about it, almost all the significant advancements that civilization has made are because someone ventured out to break from tradition.

Most people saw nothing wrong with slavery and it has been a part of human civilization from the start of known history, yet when someone stood up to say that this was wrong, there was a paradigm shift. The same with the principle of the world being flat and with the principle of the earth being the center of the universe.

This could be the same with our method of execution for personal growth. Maybe no one has ever tried the approach you are thinking about. But what if you are right? What if you can speed up the process by using the method that you'd like to try? My friend, you'll never know unless you try.

Adjusting your method to gain traction in personal development is always a difficult decision to make. As humans, we have the tendency to stick to the old and beaten road that others have already taken. However, if you want to create your own path, then you must be willing to shift your thinking and develop new paradigms. The cost might be great, but who knows, maybe the reward is even greater!

3. Adjust Your Motivation

At the beginning of this chapter, I highlighted how our motivation will eventually wane and how it affects our pursuit for personal development. Though I believe that having the tenacity to stay in the process even after the initial inspiration is already gone, I am still a big believer when it comes to the power of motivation in a person's life. Will Rogers states, *"Even if you're on the right track, you'll get run over if you just sit there."* That is why adjusting your motivation is also important. Consider these suggestions to adjust your motivation.

a. Find the right Anchor

Motivation wanes when it is tied up with something that is short-lived. For instance, most people are hyped up when they attend a seminar and hear an inspiring message from a great motivational speaker. However, as they go home and face the reality of their lives, their fire from the event will eventually fade out. Why is that? Because the motivation is based on a short-lived anchor that is the event.

When the euphoria of the event is gone, when you don't see the speaker anymore, when your friends are away from you, then the desire for change is also gone. How to fix this?

Simple. Find the right anchor for your motivation. Well, it's not simple because it involves a lot of soul-searching and reflection.

What is an example of a good anchor? It must be very dear to your heart. *Why do you want to start a business?* Being rich is not a good anchor, but being able to provide for all the needs of your family might be. *Why do you want to improve yourself?* Being popular is not a good anchor, but being able to touch lives and make impact to other people might be. What is a good anchor for you?

b. *Transform motivation from an emotion into a decision*

Emotions come and go. You might be inspired today, but you might feel dejected tomorrow. If you base your motivation on shifting emotions, then you are headed for disaster. I once heard someone say, *"Don't make promises when you are happy and don't make decisions when you are angry."* That makes a lot of sense, because human emotions are unstable at best. No matter how good you are in suppressing them, your emotions will eventually show and reveal what's truly in your heart.

For this reason, an individual who is serious in personal development must not rely on his emotions to 'feel' motivated. No, your motivation must come from something deeper, something stronger, and something firmer. And that could be a well-thought decision. I love how Ralph Waldo Emerson puts it. He said, *"Once you make a decision, the universe conspires to make it happen."*

Motivation will always be an important element of any endeavor in life, especially when you pursue personal development. However, when motivation fails, let the decisions that you made be the foundation where you build your actions.

Don't fall into the trap of not doing things because you don't 'feel' like doing them. Joyce Meyer says it better: *"Go beyond what you feel like doing and do what's right. Every time you do what's right when you don't feel like it, you are growing."*

Make Your Expectations Your Reality

U.S. President Abraham Lincoln once said, *"The best way to predict your future is to create it."* It is a universal truth in life that most of the time, expectations differ from reality. There is no guarantee or any assurance that you can make to do otherwise. However, it doesn't mean that you should stop expecting. Without expectation, then there is nothing to look forward to. And that is not the ideal life that you would want for yourself.

"Whatever you strongly expect, and deeply entertain in your heart, creates your reality, so, be mindful what you think about daily" – Chindah Chindah

Whatever it is that you want to accomplish when it comes to personal development and self-improvement, just remember this rule of thumb: *Do your best to control the things you can control and learn to live with those things that you can't.* Your expectations can become your reality once you admit that cold-hard truth and live in the principle of adjustment. Create plans for your life, but give allowance for adjustments along the way. That is one of the best ways to pursue personal development.

Discussion Questions and Reflections:

This portion of each chapter aims to establish the concepts and principles that you have learned so far. Try to carefully consider each question and answer it with a complete reflection of how it applies to your life. I would also implore you to take notes and even share what you have learned with others to initiate healthy discussion.

1. Upon embarking on the journey of personal development, what are the harsh realities that you could encounter? Have you experienced the waning of initial motivation? How did you respond? What do you usually do when you feel overwhelmed by everything that you need to do? What do you think is the best way to combat this?

   _____

   _____

2. In the chapter, we have discussed the five most common responses of people when it comes to *"Expectations ≠ Reality";* what is your usual response regarding this? Out of the four negative responses, what do you think is the most damaging? How do you think *re-evaluating* can help when it comes to responding to change?

   _____

   _____

3. The Principle of Adjustment is a necessary part of achieving your goal and as part of the process of personal development. Out of the three areas that were mentioned – namely skills, method, and motivation – what is the area that you struggle the most with? What steps will you take to bridge the gap between your expectations and the reality you are currently living?

   _____

   _____

   _____

ESTABLISHING BEHAVIOR

CHAPTER 7

*"Behavior is the mirror in which
everyone shows their image."*

– John Wolfgang von Goethe

What is the unquestionable sign of growth? How can you say that a person is developing and maturing in terms of his personality and character? What is the evidence that a person is transitioning from the old version to the new version of himself? I believe there is one answer to all these questions – behavior. Behavior is an important aspect of an individual's personality. You can talk all you want and say all the words to justify that you are changing for the better, but in the end, your behavior will show if what you are saying is true. Emily Dickinson quipped, *"Behavior is what a man does, not what he thinks, feels, or believes."*

"Your behaviors and attitudes are significant to your progress, so as not to miss your altitude in life" – Chindah Chindah

Since behavior is a crucial aspect in measuring the personal growth of a person, it is also essential to determine the factors affecting it. Unfortunately, all of us project our current behaviors based on past information that happened in our lives. If you are afraid to speak in public, perhaps you have experienced some form of humiliation when you were still a kid. If you are quite rude in your dealings with other people, then maybe you acquired these characteristics from the way adults behaved when you were still young. However, despite roots that can be traced back, the effects of our behaviors can last for a lifetime. It affects our current life, the way people perceive us, and the way we see the world around us.

If you felt victimized by some form of self-destructive behavior, then you know that it's high time for you to experience change. And I hope that by reading this book, you are slowly but surely gaining traction in this aspect of yourself. In this chapter, we will focus more on the topic of behavior. We will begin by gaining a deeper understanding of the concept and ideas surrounding behavior, including a detailed discussion of its source and how you can leverage it. Next, we will discuss the principle of clear direction and how it can affect the behavior of an individual. Lastly, we will focus on the concept of nurturing a behavior. The process of nurturing is a natural approach that we have been doing ever since we gained understanding. However, it doesn't identify between dysfunctional and right behavior and thus, the need to take control of the nurturing process.

A Victim of Behavior

Do you know that in some forms of measurement, men take better care of themselves compared to women? In fact, according to a study, men are generally in better health compared to the members of the opposite sex. Men are also less likely to be fat and are less likely to suffer chronic diseases like diabetes, osteoporosis, and arthritis.

In addition to better physical and medical health, men have also a lower tendency to experience depression compared to their female counterpart. However, despite all these surprising statistics, men are generally more prone to die sooner compared to women. The average life span of guys is seven years shorter than women.

One reason being cited for this phenomenon is the propensity of men to exhibit self-destructive behaviors. Men are more likely to be alcoholics and drug addicts. Men are also far more likely to die in a vehicular accident compared to women. With regards to the outcomes of life, boys have a greater tendency to end up in prison or be thrown out of school because of poor behavior. A psychologist at Harvard Medical School, William S. Pollack said, *"Between boys' suicide rates, dropout rates, and homicide rates, and men's self-destructive behaviors generally, we have a real crisis in America."* For the longest course of time, men fall victim to their behaviors. And something must be done about it.

Defining Behavior

If behavior can spell life or death for an individual, then we must give more attention to it than providing it with just a cursory glance. We need to understand it deeper and see its real effect in the life of a person. Dr. Steve Maraboli insightfully commented, *"If a person does it often, it isn't a mistake; it's just his behavior."* If you want to correct your life, then don't look at the situation around you, look at the behavior inside you that is being displayed outside of you.

Behavior is defined in the dictionary as *"the way in which one acts or conducts oneself, especially toward others."* Another source defines it as *"the way in which an animal or person acts in response to a particular situation or stimulus."* In a more scientifically sounding description, human behavior is defined as *"the array of every physical action and observable emotion associated with individuals, as well as humans as a whole."* Based on these definitions, we can identify some important points when it comes to the concept of behavior:

a. *Behavior is a display of action or emotions*

The way you act is your behavior and the way you show how you feel is also your behavior. These are external displays of what's inside you. You are confident in the way you talk because you know what you are talking about. You are rude to the waiter in the restaurant because you believe you are higher compared to her. You are slow in the task that you are doing because you don't want to be pressured. All these things can be seen in the way you act and that's how you observe a person's behavior.

b. *Behavior is caused by a stimulus*

Your inner behavior will be displayed once there is a stimulus that triggers it. For instance, most people think that having a lot of money changes a person. However, money doesn't change the person, it only reveals the true behavior of that individual when it comes to wealth. Another example would be a gentle girl who suddenly becomes angered because of someone who might take advantage of her.

c. *Behavior is generally involuntary*

Since our behaviors flow out from the inside, which can be triggered by outside factors, we display it – generally – in an involuntary manner. You can try to suppress your sadness, but it will always find its way out. You might say that you are happy with the success of your rival, but if you envy him on the inside, then it will eventually be displayed without you knowing it.

There's a classic story that illustrates this point impressively. A boy was reprimanded by his mother because of his naughty antics. Same with kids his age, he sought attention from his parents by doing mischievous stuff. However, it did not sit well with his mom so she scolded him and said, *"That's enough, Malcolm! You sit over there in that chair or I will whack you with this spatula!"* The boy grudgingly went over to the chair and sat as his mom said. After a couple of minutes, he said to his mother, *"Mom. I'm sitting on the outside. But I'm standing on the inside."*

Yes, your behavior is always being displayed in the way you act and the way you show your emotions. You can't hide it. You can't live with integrity outside what's really going on inside you. In fact, I will be bold enough to say that if you are behaving badly, then it's not the behavior that you need to fix, but the motivation, the feelings, and the emotions sitting inside your inner most self.

Digging the Source of Behavior

Behavior is like a fever. In medical parlance, a fever is not really the problem per se, but it indicates that something is wrong in your body. It is the same with our behaviors. Your rudeness, pride, envy, etc. are not the real problem with you, it only shows that there is a deeper problem that you need to address inside you and thus, the need to dig deeper to understand the true source of our behavior. Don't waste your time fixing what can be seen by other people. You can't cure your insolence by trying now and then to be considerate with other people. You can't remove your pride by exercising false humility. And you can't extinguish your envy without properly addressing your scarcity mindset. All the destructive behaviors that you display are just the *"fever"* shown outside; the objective now is to identify the real source of these signs so we can address them accordingly.

The great philosopher, Plato, once said, *"Human behavior flows from three main sources: desire, emotion, and knowledge."* I know that the study of human behavior is much more complicated than that. In fact, we have a separate branch of science that deals with this aspect of human life and interaction. Thus, I believe issuing a caveat is appropriate. The concepts and ideas that will be discussed here are limited only to the perception and understanding of the author of available facts with regards to human behavior. The teachings written do not pretend or aim to be interpreted as medical dogma and therefore should not be treated as such.

Going back to the quotation from Plato, I believe that behavior – the visible way of how we act and interact with others – is based on those three progressive sources. First is the knowledge, which will produce desire and consequently bear the fruit of emotions. Let me elaborate on each aspect:

a. Knowledge

Our actions are primarily defined by the things that we know. If you know that there will be an examination tomorrow, then perhaps you will drive yourself to study your lessons all night. If you know your wife is cheating on you, then your actions will be hostile towards her. Our knowledge is the main source of our motivation and will, thus the central source of our behavior patterns are the things that we know.

Let's face it, the knowledge that we have always determines the way that we act. In fact, even the lack of knowledge can drive you to act in certain ways of avoiding those unknown factors. The things taught to us by our parents, teachers, and the books that we read have formed our intellect, on which we based our behaviors. It's the same thing with our experiential

113

knowledge. The things we underwent – receiving honor in school, embarrassment in a public place, being left behind by friends – also form the body of knowledge inside our minds.

The knowledge forms the foundation for what we believe is truc and builds paradigms and perspectives about the way we see the world. The problem here is when the knowledge that we have is faulty or erroneous as opposed to reality. If the knowledge that you have is wrong, then your behavior will be wrong also. Interracial interactions can provide a great illustration for this concept. For instance, the people in France consider kissing on both cheeks as an acceptable form of greeting. However, in Asian countries like China, a polite nod is what they consider appropriate since they are more conservative. Now, imagine the disaster that could happen when a French man, without knowledge of Chinese customs, greets a Chinese lady!

b. *Desire*

Thc knowledge you acquire over time, will largely influence the desires that develops inside you. If you believe that money is the most important thing in the world and is the only way for you to experience lasting happiness, then guess what you will desire it? Now, based on that desire, you will act and behave intentionally to make more money. In the same way, if you learn and believe that people are there to make your life miserable, then there is a great possibility that you will desire and do everything in your power to be alone.

The knowledge that we have becomes the basis for our desires, and the inner desires that we have manifest in the way we behave. However, there are times that the complexity of our desires might cause an erratic display in our behavior. M. Scott Peck, author of *The Road Less Travelled,* expressed that same sentiment. He said, *"The difficulty that we have in accepting responsibility for our behavior lies in the desire to avoid the pain of the consequences of that behavior."* In other words, there is a desire to do, and a desire to flee.

However, the main principle stands true: *What you desire*

determines how you behave. And depending on the intensity of your desire is the magnitude of the actions that you will take. Think about it: who are the most competitive when it comes to sports? Normally, it's those people who are the hungriest win. You see, their desires are being displayed in the way they play. This is true of sports and other arenas of life.

c. ***Emotions***

Once you have the knowledge, and the knowledge produces the desire, the next thing that will present are the emotions that accompany both. Let us try to illustrate it in a simple analogy. Imagine you were so busy doing your office tasks that you forgot to eat your lunch. Now, after a few more hours, you hear the rumbling of your stomach and you remember, *"My gosh! I forgot to eat my lunch."* Upon realizing this you now have the desire to eat lunch and satisfy your hunger. However, upon looking at your bag, you realize that you forgot your lunchbox at home. Now, the desire to eat and the additional knowledge that you don't have food will naturally trigger an emotion. The emotion that will manifest will depend on your personality and character. And the way you respond, the way you act out of the frustration, and the way you handle it, is your behavior.

I believe that the way we handle these kinds of circumstances reveals the true state of our maturity and growth. If you are angry with the world and express your frustration by being rude to other people, then perhaps your behavior points towards an aspect of your personality that you need to address.

Now, does it mean that you need to always act nice despite what you are going through? The answer is, depending on your level of maturity. Remember, the way you behave is just like a *"fever"* that wants to point out the deeper issues about yourself.

If our behavior can make or break you when it comes to treating ourselves and interacting with other people, then it is crucial to carefully evaluate its sources. We need to have a keen eye in observing the way we behave and watch out for red flags that might signal a deeper problem inside. This principle should also bring you to a realization that the best way to deal with destructive and dysfunctional behaviors is by intently looking at our minds and examining our paradigms against established and timeless principles of life.

Qualities of an Ideal Behavior

Now that we have identified the different sources of the way we behave, it is time to describe the different qualities of an ideal behavior. Though, I must admit that displaying a perfect behavior might be impossible for any normal human, there are still some safeguards that an individual can use to strengthen those areas where his behavior is most susceptible to being destructive. At the same time, our behaviors can spell success or failure in all our endeavors, therefore taking responsibility of it is crucial to what we will accomplish. Dr. Steve Maraboli pulled off an amazing insight about this idea. He said, *"Be + Have = Behave. You will experience your success when you behave accordingly. Be and you shall Have."*

a. *An ideal behavior reflects timeless principles*

Stephen Covey outlined in his book, *"The 7 Habits of Highly Effective People"*, the importance of principles when it comes to our lives. According to the late author, there are timeless principles that govern human interaction for effective living. These principles have been present since the dawn of human civilization and have propelled nations towards progress or extinction.

For instance, the principles of fairness and equality, love, belief, responsibility, and others, can help individuals unleash the maximum potential of their lives and at the same time create a maximum impact in the lives of other people. If your behavior reflects these timeless principles – if you take responsibility for your own life and actions, if you treat other people as human being who deserves equality, if you do to others the things you want them to do you – then you have ideal behavior.

116

b. *Ideal behavior mirrors reality but considers possibilities*

We have discussed earlier that the primary source of the way we behave is knowledge we acquired over the years and used to build the foundation for our beliefs. Because of this principle, it is important to ensure that the knowledge that we acquired is close to the actual realities of life. If you acquire knowledge that makes you successful without doing anything, then that will produce harmful behaviors in your life and you end up disappointed. Why? Because the knowledge is not based on reality.

In the same way, if you build your life on the belief that success is impossible to achieve, then the way you behave will also be detrimental to your life. Again, it is because the knowledge that bears the behavior is also faulty. Yes, you must always consider reality, however it is equally important to look at the possibilities. Yes, maybe achieving success is hard right now, but the possibility of achieving it is always there. Hence you should act in a way that will bring you to that desired destination in the future.

c. *An ideal behavior is not just about you*

The way you behave is an issue about yourself. No other person can take responsibility to fix those faulty behaviors, except you. However, even if you oversee your behavior, the way you act will always affect the lives of people around you. For instance, you might tell yourself after reading this that you don't have to fix your behavior about being a chronically angry person. That's the way you are and you can do nothing about it, right? Yet, I want you to ask yourself: *"When I am angry, do I hurt other people, too? Physically or emotionally?"*

An ideal behavior considers the impact of the way you behave with the lives of other people, especially those who are closest to you. You don't have to be a wrecking ball who is trying to destroy everything that is standing in its way. You can be the glue that uses your skills to glue people together because of what you do for them.

There are other characteristics that might define the ideal behavior of an individual; however, these three concepts are enough to bring you to new heights once you take responsibility for the way you behave. Remember, your behavior is always your responsibility and no one can bring out the worst in you unless you let them. Do your best to develop these ideal behaviors and in time, you will reap the rewards of your labor by doing yourself and other people some good in their lives.

The Concept of Direction

Cultivating the right behavior will be a wasted effort if you do not do your part in establishing a clear direction first. The previous chapters of this book helped you to set the right course towards your desired destination with *change* as your anchor. However, in this section, we will delve deeper in the concept of direction and how it can affect our lives. As Chinese philosopher, Lao Tzu, insightfully said, *"If you do not change direction, you may end up where you are heading."* Are you on the right track right now?

In simple terms, direction is where you are headed and it's the path where you are currently moving. Without a clear direction, you are liable to be lost. Without the right direction, you are liable to fail in what you are trying to achieve. But with the right direction, you can go faster where you want to go. However, before you can determine if you are moving in the right direction, you need first to determine where you want to go in the first place. What is it that you are trying to achieve? How do you see yourself in the future? After you have settled these matters, then you can start to move confidently towards your dreams.

Henry David Thoreau said, *"I have learned that if one advances confidently in the direction of his dreams, and endeavors to live the life he has imagined, he will meet with a success unexpected in common hours."* If you have a clear destination, then setting the right course will be easier. But this is not enough. You need to continuously move towards that path if you want to arrive at that set target. That is the importance of having a clear direction!

Direction and Behavior

Now, you might be thinking, *"What the heck is the connection of having the right direction with the topic of behavior?"* And to that I will say that there is a deep and profound relationship between the two. In fact, they are so closely related that one is useless without the other. Let me illustrate. Imagine for a minute you are a football player running across the field with the ball at your disposal. Now, you have a set destination and the direction to run towards it. But what if you run slowly and do not guard the ball well? You know that there is now a great possibility your opponent will steal the ball. You see, having the right direction is not enough. You must also have the right behavior to display while walking in that specific direction.

The reverse is also true. Again, let's go back to the football player example earlier. Imagine yourself moving faster than any other player on the field and you guard the ball so exceptionally well that no opponent can get it from you. In short, your behavior while playing is extremely good.

However, you can't see the goal anywhere and it dawns on you that everything you are doing will just be wasted because you don't know where to put that ball to score. No matter how well you behave, if you don't know your destination or what you truly want to accomplish, then everything will be for naught.

Both direction and behavior are essential for success in this life. You can't continue exhibiting a high-performance if you don't have a clear direction, and you are bound to live in mediocrity if you display average behavior when it comes to accomplishing your goals.

However, having the combination of clear direction and exceptional behavior will boost your chances of experiencing success in your life. You just have to decide right now where you want to *"be"* and do your best to *"have"* what it takes. In other words, just *behave.*

Revisiting your Direction

The directions that we set for ourselves do not stay consistently the same on their own. There are distractions and things that aim to move us out of concentration and focus. And before we know it we are speeding fast towards a different direction. What are the goals that you have set for yourself? What are the different aspects of your life that you determined to change? Are you still doing things that are closely related to what you originally wanted to accomplish? Or do you find yourself pursuing different things and moving in several directions at the same time?

Jim Rohn insightfully said, "*You cannot change your destination overnight, but you can change your direction overnight.*" This principle can work both in a positive or negative manner. If you are initially headed to the wrong destination, then you don't need to wait for a major event to happen just to change your direction –, you can change it overnight if you want to. In the same way, if you are already moving towards the right destination, you might want to revisit your direction because it can easily change if you are not aware. Here are some things that you might want to consider when you revisit your direction:

1. Revisit your motivation

Your '*why*' is a very powerful force that can shift your life from passionless existence to a purposeful pursuit of goals. However, our reasons or motivations for doing certain things might be different if they are not established properly. Revisiting your motivation means asking yourself if your reason for behaving in a certain way is still the same reason that got you started in the first place. If not, then you must take note what caused the change and if it was for the better.

For instance, imagine that you decided to lose some weight this year because you want to stay healthy for your family. After a few months, you might feel demotivated and losing weight might seem like a drag. Now, you need to revisit your motivation. Why are you still trying to lose weight? Is it because of your original reason of staying healthy for your family? Or is it now because you don't want to look like a quitter, which means that your pride is your new motivation?

2. Revisit your commitment

Commitment is strong when things are getting started. Everyone is excited to live their lives differently. Everyone is willing to pay the cost and sacrifice for the benefit of achieving their goals. However, as time goes by, the flame of commitment slowly reduces to a flicker of light just waiting to be snuffed out. So, you should ask yourself, *"Am I still committed to the cause like the way I was before?"* If not, then you must carefully reflect on the reason why.

I read a quote somewhere that said, *"Commitment means staying loyal to what you said you were going to do, long after the mood you said it has left you."* That is right, my friend. Most people set their commitments based on their moods. Don't let that be you.

3. Revisit your behavior

Are the actions that you are doing still consistent and in line with the goal that you are trying to achieve? Is the way you behave right now still reflecting the initial motivation and direction that you have set for yourself? As we have discussed earlier, human behavior flows from our knowledge, which gives birth to desire and transforms it into emotions.

The way you do things and the way you respond to your emotions are crucial because those things are what get you to your goal. It is the vehicle that moves you in a set direction and if the vehicle is modified and moves in another direction, then you might not accomplish what you originally set for yourself.

Direction is not consistent unless you intentionally revisit it often to correct any deviation from the charted course. You cannot expect that your motivation, commitment and behavior will stay as is because change is always happening in your life. You need to be proactive enough to sit down and evaluate if you are still moving in the right direction and if not, then take the appropriate actions to get you back on track.

Nurturing Newly Acquired Behaviors

If you have taken seriously the challenge in the previous chapters to embrace change to improve yourself, then I believe you have acquired some new behaviors that aim to help you in doing just that. Perhaps you have a new way of thinking when it comes to your current situation, or maybe you have instituted a new way to act towards achieving your goals. Whatever it is,you must also ensure that you can nurture those behaviors in order to make it part of yourself. Your goal is to let those behaviors be an involuntary response to stimuli in your inner and outside environment. Here are some tips to get you started:

1. Establish Habits and Routines

Habits are defined according to Cambridge English Disctionary, as the things that we repeatedly do and often we are not aware of them. They are also defined by Sean Covey, an American Author and motivational speaker, as a *"constant, often unconscious inclination to perform an act, acquired through its frequent repetition."*

Routines are also identical in the way that they pertain to those things or activities that we repeatedly and consistently do. Habits and routines are the skeleton of our behavior. Even if you are aware or not, our behaviors are being displayed by the things we constantly do – that is our habits and routines.

There are three elements of a habit, and if you want to create and establish new habits then you must take control of these three elements. Now, my friend, if you have tried changing a bad habit or instituting a good habit before, then you know how hard it is. However, it doesn't mean that it is impossible. It might be difficult at first, but you can certainly do it in time if you want to. Let what Henry David Thoreau said inspire you: *"I know of no more encouraging fact than the unquestionable ability of man to elevate his life by conscious endeavor."*

Going back, here are the three elements of a habit that you need to identify and institute if you want to establish a new habit:

1. The Trigger

This element is what initiates a habit. It could be a specific time, a condition, or an event that signals that you need to do a certain activity. For instance, if you want to create a habit of reading a book for an hour a day, then you need a specific cue that will indicate that you need to do it. Let us say for example that your trigger is a specific time of the day.

You set five o' clock in the evening as your cue. That means at 5' o clock every evening, you need to stop everything that you are doing, grab your book and start reading it.

You can also use a condition. For example, instead of using five o' clock in the evening as your trigger, you may decide to use the condition *"after taking a bath."* That means that every time that you finish bathing, you need to get your book and start to read.

2. The Act

The act pertains to the specific actions that you need to take – this is the specific habit that you need to perform or develop. In the example above, the act is the activity to read a book. However, to make it more powerful and effective, then be specific in the details of your action. For instance, you can specify the title of the book and the number of hours or pages that you intend to read every day.

You can also set an overall goal and break it into manageable actions that you can do consistently. Let's say for example that your goal is to read a book every month. Then you just should divide that goal in terms of days and this will be the basis for your habit.

3. The Why

This element is the most important part of a habit. Without a potent *"why"*, the habits that you try to establish will crumble in the demands of your daily life. Your habits must be anchored in a profound foundation therefore you must think carefully of your *"why"*.

Going back to our example earlier, ask yourself, *"Why do I want to read a book every day?"* Then start listing all the reasons you can think of. Pick one to three of the most powerful reasons you can think of and let those reasons be your *"why."*

2. Establish Principles to Live By

I have discussed in the earlier part of this chapter the importance of building your behavior on sound and timeless principles. I believe it is worth repeating here in the closing words of this chapter. In his best-selling book, *"The 7 Habits of Highly Effective People,"* Stephen Covey defined principles as *"guidelines for human conduct that are proven to have enduring, permanent value. They're fundamental. They're essentially unarguable because they are self-evident."*

When we talk about principles, these are the things that you base your behaviors on if you want them to endure. Because the principles are timeless and enduring, then it is only logical that you base your actions and the way you interact with others on these lest you just set yourself up for a huge disappointment.

Let me illustrate. Say for instance you have decided to build a behavior that gives you the capacity to learn new things every day. Based on that behavior you want to cultivate a habit of reading a book for an hour every day. However, your desire to learn is based on the principle of revenge. You want to get back at those people who have humiliated you before so you want to gain knowledge and be successful so you can spit in their faces with your achievements. Now, we all know that anger and revenge won't do you any good. You might be successful in achieving your dreams, but you might also lose yourself in the process. At the same time, your revenge to those people will also breed revenge in their hearts which can run for generations after you.

Now think about this: what if your behavior is anchored on the principle of helping other people? Then you can have a more positive impact in the lives of others. Your impact will multiply as those people that you could help will also help others to improve themselves. And in time, your influence will grow rapidly that you leave a lasting legacy in this world. That is the power of being

124

anchored in timeless principles of effective living.

3. Establish a Plan for Progressive Behavior

Human behavior doesn't remain static. It grows and develops depending on the acquisition of new knowledge, stirring up new desires and bearing new emotions. The good news is that, this change is not an addition, it's a multiplication. The good behavior that you have acquired will compound to better behaviors in the future. However, there is still the possibility of going back to your old ways and patterns.

Therefore, you must take control of the process of change and establish a plan towards a progressive behavior.

For instance, if you are cultivating the behavior of being a lifelong learner and student of life, and you decide to develop the habit of consistently reading a book every day, then you can progress that behavior to be a lifelong teacher of others in the future. Create a plan for how you can implement it by finding other people who have a similar need and interest and guide them through the process. By doing this, you let your knowledge flow to other individuals which can also be compounded when they teach it to other people.

Your only limit is yourself. One of the principles that I love is the principle of growth. It is the idea that we are embryonic and have the capacity to develop, acquire new skills, learn new things, and release more and more potential. In fact, this principle is the very foundation of this book. The concept of self-improvement is anchored on that principle and if you are serious enough to walk that path, then I can guarantee you that you will unleash your greatest potential. I would like to encourage you to build and nurture a behavior based on the principle of growth.

"If you are not growing in all areas of your life, then you are dying in those areas of your life slowly" – Chindah Chindah

125

The Key to Establishing Behavior

As I have said earlier, trying to change your old ways and pattern of thinking is a difficult process. Most people end up going back to what they know instead of embracing change and doing their best to develop and improve themselves. Establishing behavior carries the same struggle. However, there is a specific key that you can use to do it. It is by being purposely stubborn and having the unwavering persistence to continue the pursuit.

Decide beforehand that you won't allow yourself to quit and give up no matter how hard the process will be. If you are being distracted, just remember the reason why you got started in the first place. Find a higher purpose in everything you do. Pursue something that is bigger than yourself. Live a vision that is greater than what you can accomplish on your own. And let that purpose, aspirations, and vision fuel your desire for change and motivate you to stay on track as you establish habits, routines, and progressive behaviors. As Sir Winston Churchill once said, *"Never, never, never give up."*

Discussion Questions and Reflections:

This portion of each chapter aims to establish the concepts and principles that you have learned so far. Try to carefully consider each question and answer it with a complete reflection of how it applies to your life. I would also implore you to take notes and even share what you have learned with others to initiate healthy discussion.

1. Describe in your own words your current behavior now. Is your current behavior helping you or distracting you in achieving your goals in life, particularly around self-improvement? Of the three sources of behavior, do you believe that knowledge is the most important? Why or why not? What destructive behavior do you have that is hampering your momentum to unleash potential in your life? What do you plan to do about it?

_____

_____

_____

2. After reading several chapters of this book, do you see yourself moving in the right direction now? Why or why not? If you are now headed in the right direction, what do you think is the best way you can stay on this path? In your own words, discuss the importance of constantly revisiting your direction. What is the result of this practice when it comes to the area of improving yourself?

_____

_____

_____

3. What helpful habits have you developed over time that help you right now in improving yourself? What additional habits do you want to add to your life to propel you towards accomplishing your goals? What destructive habits do you

want to remove and how do you intend to remove it? List 10 principles that you believe can help you in establishing helpful behaviors that can fast track your pursuit of success. Do you have a plan to cultivate a progressive behavior? Use the S-M-A-R-T method to carefully lay down your plans and goals.

_____

_____

_____

THE SECRET TO BEING LIMITLESS

CHAPTER 8

*"There is no passion to be found in playing
small – in settling for a life that is less than the
one that you are capable of living."*

– Nelson Mandela

You see them everywhere. The most visible of them are those who play sports. You might also spot them when watching your favorite movies. Some of them are in offices and you briefly see them '*shine*' during planning or other meetings. Maybe you saw some of them at your school, in your community, or at your religious center. Do you know what I'm talking about? I'm talking about passionate people. They are everywhere and it is my sincere hope that you will be one of them. Why? Because I believe that passion – the intense kind of passion – is the secret to being limitless.

"Everyone is naturally designed to be passionate about something. So, discover your passion, and separate yourselves from the crowd" – Chindah Chindah

All of us have this inner desire to get out of the box. All of us, in different moments in our lives, wished for freedom – freedom to do whatever we want, freedom to pursue our dreams, and freedom to make our visions a reality. However, only a handful of people have the courage to do it and remove any barriers that hinder them from doing what they love to do.

Those people are people with passion. They follow the inner

voice inside them. It doesn't matter what life throws at them because they believe that the only way to live is if they stay true to where their heart is.

This chapter is dedicated to help you discover that passion of yours and help you to turn that passion into an immovable force that will help you to move past the boundaries that are being set for you by your family, peers, and society. Who says you are just meant to rot in your cubicle in the office? Who dare lecture you that you don't have what it takes to make a difference? Who is brave enough to stop you unleashing your potential? No one! Unless you let other people do it to you.

This chapter aims to spark that passion inside you and show you how you can further cultivate it. It also includes three stories of people who lived with unwavering passion, made a significant difference in the lives of millions of people, and left the world a better place. Lastly, this chapter will discuss the three steps that you can follow to have the secret to be limitless – passion.

The Cave Digger's Passion

Rau Paulette is a 76-year-old sculptor with a unique fondness for turning caves into beautiful works of art. One could say that this old man has an unusual passion. For over 30 years now, Paulette has been digging cave after cave and filling these lifeless stone shelters with paintings, pools, skylights, furniture and waterfalls. Using only a pickaxe, a scraper and a wheelbarrow, Paulette is revolutionizing the way art can be perceived by sense.

Paulette was featured in a documentary entitled *"Cavedigger"* to which he was interviewed plenty of times. The director Jeffrey Karoff followed Paulette into one of the caves as he carved the rocks and started working his craft. In an interview, Paulette said, *"When I'm working on a project, I'm totally obsessed. I'm thinking about it all day long. All night long, I'm dreaming... digging dreams. Most people who are engaged in physical labor aren't having the fun that I'm having."*

Rau Paulette, is an old cave digger. However, he is so passionate that all you can think is, *"What's wrong with this guy?"* Can he inspire us. And his lifework can conjure the question, *"What about me? What is my passion?"* Discovering and harnessing your passion is one of the greatest favors that you can give to yourself. Living a life that is not dedicated or at least not about what you really love to do, is a life that is lived less that its potential. However, with passion, you can live a fulfilling and impactful life. German philosopher, Georg Wilhelm Friedrich Hegel said it succinctly: *"Nothing great in the world has ever been accomplished without passion."*

What is Passion?

In order to harness its power in our lives and make us limitless, first, we need to carefully understand what passion is. Passion is defined in the Merriam-Webster dictionary " Imagine Rau Paulette waking up every morning, excited to go in one of those dimly lit caves to continue working on his project.

As he shovels the earth out and chisels the lime stones, he is smiling while thinking about the finished product of this masterpiece. How about you?

Passion is not just about being happy in what you do. The intensity of enthusiasm and excitement must be strong to the point that you can't let your day be finished without doing that activity. Passion is being involved, engaged and in some ways, obsessed with working on a project. When you wake up, all you can think about is all the things that you can add to your project and when you are in your bed, all you can think about is what you will do tomorrow. That is passion. And when you have this kind of emotion, you can do almost anything.

I saw a quotation that beautifully captured the idea of passion. It said:

"Passion is not only a strong feeling, it is actually a kind of crazed fervor that gets you going. Passion is all about that driving force that moves every one of your feelings and makes you feel euphorically alive."

Benefits of a Passion

Passion avails those who are brave enough to pursue it with a lot of advantages and benefits. First, passion enables those individuals to do things that dispassionate people won't do. Passion also gives them the strength that they need to overcome obstacles and hurdles that hinder them in doing those things that they love to do.

Passion also gives a tremendous boost when everything is going slow. If you still don't know what your passion is, then it's high time that you did what you can to find it. Here are some other benefits that can motivate you to live out your passion.

1. Passion is an important ingredient of success

Imagine that there are two employees working on two tasks with the same difficulty level. The first employee goes about his work with less than inspiring enthusiasm. He seems really bored at everything that is going on and is just waiting for the clock to hit five o'clock so he can go home. Also, while doing his tasks, he constantly looks at his phone just to pass time in social media. At best, you could describe the first employee as dispassionate about what he is doing.

On the other hand, the second employee goes about his work with a lot of infectious enthusiasm. He seems happy and excited about everything that is going on to the point that he is not aware of how fast time runs. If possible, he wants to work for another one to two hours because he is just excited about what he is doing. Also, he is extremely focused and concentrated on the task at hand. At best, you could describe the second employee as a passionate guy doing what he loves to do and loving what he is doing.

Now, all things being equal, who do you think will succeed in getting a promotion? When you are passionate, you increase your odds of success. Why? Because you love what you are doing. And because of this love, you don't treat work as drag, but rather a joy. Apple co-founder, Steve Jobs, pointed out: *"The only way to be truly satisfied is to do what you believe is great work. And the only way to do great work is to love what you do."*

2. Passion makes you more alive

Passion is like a machine that turns your potential into usable energy.

Therefore, if you don't have passion, most of the potential hidden inside you will remain stagnant and unusable. However, when you love what you are doing, the potential that you have is released and it gives you the strength you need to continue, no matter how difficult the task at hand is. You don't differentiate between playing and working, because you are both enjoying those activities. Someone once said,

"Working hard for something we don't care about is called stress. Working hard for something we love is called passion."

Isn't it true? I recently saw the movie *La La Land* where the male protagonist is a passionate pure jazz player. He really loves jazz music and has dreamed of establishing a jazz club of his own where only jazz music will be played.

However, because of the need to support himself and pay the rent, he was forced to join a band that played punk music. And imagine the dismay on his face as he plays his keyboard along with the rest of the band. That is what happens when we do things that we don't care about. We look alive, but inside, we are slowly dying.

3. Passion produces excellence

Excellence means that you are so good at what you do. Now, there are some people who are naturally gifted at doing certain things. They are excellent at singing, dancing, painting, leading, and other tasks that are difficult for other people. So, what if you are just average at doing a particular craft? Do you still have the hope of developing excellence? I believe you do. However, your shot at excellence will be largely determined by the passion that you have.

Think about this: how can you be so good at something you do, if you don't love what you are doing? It is nonsense. And unless you are naturally gifted in doing it, you can't expect any significant progress in your excellence if you don't have passion for it. As Ralph Waldo Emerson said, *"Nothing great was ever achieved without enthusiasm."*

If you are not passionate, then you are missing a lot. You might be missing your potential to be successful in whatever endeavor that you put your hands to. You might be missing the ability to live a more satisfied and fulfilled life.

You might also miss your shot at becoming excellent and setting the standard that others will strive for. Passion is necessary for success. Without it, you can say farewell to achieving your dreams in life.

Signs of Passion

Charles "Tremendous" Jones, once said, *"You are the same today as you'll be in five years except for two things: the books you read and the people you meet."* I personally believe that if you want to be passionate, you don't read a book but go and spend time with passionate people who are doing their best at whatever craft they are doing. So, how can we say if someone is passionate in what he does? What are the signs to look out for if we want to network and connect to those passionate people and be infected by this wonderful virus called *"passion?"*

1. Passionate people are happy

If you are doing what you love, wouldn't you be happy? If you are doing what you love and at the same time getting paid to do it, wouldn't you be happier? Passionate individuals have an infectious aura. You can see their desire to do more and accomplish more of what they are doing because they just love doing it.

However, not all happy people are passionate. There are some people that live a carefree life and don't care about anything like exerting effort and doing hard work. The happiness of passionate people is of a different kind. You can see it in the glimmer in their eyes, you can hear it in the tone of their voices, and you can feel it with the way they move!

2. Passionate people are committed

A person who is a part of an organization but doesn't really care for the vision of that organization is a dispassionate people when it comes to that aspect of his life. You can't expect him to commit to anything and you can't get him on board to all the things that the organization is doing. In meetings, his physical body might be there but he is often disengaged and already wondering what food will be served during lunch break.

On the other hand, passionate people are committed. They show up when they say they will. They do what they can do and give what they can give to accomplish the goals of the organization. Their passion is being translated to an unwavering commitment and you can sense it in the way they talk, and the way they work.

3. Passionate people are consistent

One sure sign of dispassionate people is inconsistency. There are times when he/she is good at what he does, but there are also times that you can't expect any good outcome from their work. Why? Again, because if you don't care in what you do, then you are liable to work with mediocrity in every step.

Meanwhile, passionate people can be consistent producers. They do not let outside factors affect the quality of their work, rather they use those distractions to challenge themselves to go harder. Passionate people are consistent because they find satisfaction in the work of their hands.

Passion is hard to hide. No matter what you do to conceal it, it will always find its way out and display itself for people to see. Trying to suppress passion is like trying to fit an elephant in a small house. It is hard. It is painful. It can be disastrous. If you truly love doing something, then start doing it. The world is hungry to see passionate people who have the guts to say "*no*" to the demands of society, and say "*yes*" to the things that make their hearts beat faster. John Wesley said it more beautifully. He asserted, *"Light yourself on fire with passion and people will come from miles to watch you burn."*

Passion Accounts

To further burn the idea of passion into your mind and what it can do for an individual and the lives of people around them, let us read of the stories of some of the most passionate men who lived in our world. As we read these accounts, let the beat of their hearts resonate within you and be infected by the enthusiasm of these three individuals. It is my hope that as we learn about how they were taken over by their cause, the same passion will also birth out in us.

1. Winston Churchill

Sir Winston Churchill was the prime minister of the United Kingdom from 1940– 1945, at the height of World War II. In one of the darkest periods in the history of the British people, Churchill rallied them time and again. The Axis forces with the leadership of Adolf Hitler proved to be formidable enemies. England was at the brink of defeat but Churchill led them to a great victory. In one of speeches, he said this:

> *"We have before us an ordeal of the most grievous kind. We have before us many, many long months of struggle and of suffering. You ask, what is our policy? I can say: It is to wage war, by sea, land and air, with all our might and with all the strength that God can give us; to wage war against a monstrous tyranny, never surpassed in the dark, lamentable catalogue of human crime. That is our policy. You ask, what is our aim? I can answer in one word: Victory – victory at all costs, victory in spite of terror, victory, however long and hard the road may be; for without victory, there is no survival.*

Out of the great dark clouds of fear and doubt and when they were on the brink of the most painful defeat that threatened their survival, Sir Winston Churchill saw a vision – a vision of victory – victory that would end the tyranny, the unjustified killings, and the twisted philosophy. A victory that would uphold the survival of humanity. His passion for this vision and his passion to succeed in defeating the evil forces of Hitler literally changed the course of history for humanity.

2. Martin Luther King Jr.

Racial inequality has always been a prevailing issue in America even in the 20th century. Despite the end of the civil war, the segregation and animosity between black and white people still persisted. The discrimination that was being experienced by black people pained them to the core and someone had to stand. Someone had to put an end to the century-long struggle of black people to receive equal treatment and that's when Martin Luther King, Jr. came along.

As an individual who experienced the day to day humiliation of people who had colored skin, he always believed that a person's rights should never be based on the color of their skin. With this deep discontentment with the status quo at the time, Martin Luther King Jr. became an activist and the leader of the African-American Civil Rights Movement. He started non-violent campaigns to fight for the right of the Negro people. And in one of the most monumental events in his life, in Lincoln Memorial Square which has been attended by more than 20,000 people, he communicated, from the deepest core of his soul, the vision that he had. In his legendary speech entitled, *"I Have a Dream"*, he said the following:

"I have a dream that one day this nation will rise up and live out the true meaning of its creed: 'We hold these truths to be self-evident; that all men are created equal.'

"I have a dream that my four children will one day live in a nation where they will not be judged by the color of their skin but by the content of their character.

"And when this happens, and when we allow freedom ring, when we let it ring from every village and every hamlet, from every state and every city, we will be able to speed up that day when all of God's children, black men and white men, Jews and gentiles, Protestants and Catholics, will be able to join hands and sing in the words of the old Negro spiritual,

'Free at last! Free at last! Thank God Almighty, we are free at last!'

A great dream from a great man with a great passion to see his people liberated. Martin Luther King, Jr. was assassinated on April 4, 1968 but his passion, his dream, and his vision ignited a great conflagration that consumed the hearts of the people. Today, we are all benefactors of the legacy of what he accomplished.

3. Mahatma Gandhi

Mohandas K. Gandhi, more popularly known as Mahatma Gandhi, was the primary leader of India's independence movement. He went to school in London and there he finished his law degree.

During this time, his countrymen and the entire nation of India were under the regime of the British government. Gandhi, like most Indians, dreamt of having freedom from being a British colony. They believed that they deserved it and that's why a lot of people were fighting for it in violent ways. However, Gandhi led protests and strikes around the country and promoted a non-violent civil disobedience.

Gandhi once said, *"Nonviolence is the greatest force at the disposal of mankind. It is mightier than the mightiest weapon of destruction devised by the ingenuity of man."* He was passionate about his country's freedom, but he was also passionate for peace. He challenged the Indian people to hold their ground, not by violence and force, but with peaceful disobedience and non-cooperation. There were a lot of struggles during their fight for freedom, including a massacre of the British military of one thousand people at Amritsar. Still, Gandhi commanded the people not to fight back.

His passion was indeed annoying and at the same admirable. And it proved its power when in 1947, through long years of non-violent protest and civil disobedience and because of Gandhi's leadership, India gained the right to rule itself and achieved freedom. Gandhi exemplified his beliefs and become the embodiment of his passion for his country and for his people. In one of his statements, Gandhi summarized his heartbeat and his passion: *"The best way to find yourself is to lose yourself in the service of others."*

One thing is common...

By reading through the accounts of Sir Winston Churchill, Martin Luther King, Jr. and Mahatma Gandhi, there is one common theme that is present in their lives. It is a worthy cause that captured their whole being and their passion to see it happen. If you are passionate for something, and you know in yourself that you can do excellent things by doing it, then give it a try. It doesn't need to be all-out, you just need to start somewhere. As leadership expert, John Maxwell said, *"Following your passion changes your life and the lives of those around you. It makes life exciting. It inspires your team. It transforms the grind of work into an invigorating challenge."*

Pursuing your Passion

The idea of passion goes beyond the demands of your studies, career, or social life. In fact, I am bold enough to say that if you don't know your passion, then you are not really living to the fullness of your potential. I also believe that what is in your heart sets you apart. You have a special mission, a special task to fulfill that you and only you can accomplish. Pursuing your passion is a moral responsibility. There is too much supply of complacency and mediocrity in our world and there is a shortage of passionate people. If you want to take up the challenge of pursuing your passion, then do the following:

1. Identify the Sources of Passion

Passion is not born out of thin air. You won't just wake up one day with an extraordinary enthusiasm to do something. There are different sources of passion and you must be aware of it. Also, by knowing the possible sources of passion, you will have a greater chance of discovering it in a lesser amount of time. However, you must take note that you still need to punch the timecard if you are serious in finding out what your passion is. Here are some of the sources of passion; try to look within these concepts too.

a. Talents

Let's face it, we have different talents. Some are born with voices that resonate with the voices of angels. Some have bodies that are fitted for the groove of dancing. Other individuals have the gift to turn a blank canvas into a masterpiece. And there are people with the cunning talent to learn more and more by listening to others or by reading. These are what we call talents. And for most people, their talents are a good starting point in finding out their passion.

I personally believe that what you do well can be connected to what you love to do. If you have a talent, then it can lead you towards your passion. Terry Mante quipped, *"Talent is your vehicle.*

Passion is your fuel and potential is your destination." And with regards to using your talent, poet Brendan Francis insightfully advised, *"If you have a talent, use it in every way possible. Don't hoard it. Don't dole it out like a miser. Spend it lavishly like a millionaire intent on going broke."*

b. Problems

There are some people who acquire their passion by being passionate in solving a specific problem. Their desire to make it right fuels every thought, word, and action that they make about that problem. The motivation for solving that problem varies, however, from person to person. For instance, Dashrath Manjhi, who is also known as the mountain man, became passionate about carving a mountain with only a hammer and a chisel for 22 years! The source of his resolve was after his wife died from a serious injury and the mountain became the reason why they were not able to get medical attention fast. His pain fueled his passion and because of it, he was able to carve the mountain and shorten the travel time between the blocks of his town from 55 km to 15 km.

c. *Idea*

In the movie, *Inception,* the main protagonist, Dominic Cobb, played by Leonardo DiCarpio uttered this line: *"What is the most resilient parasite? Bacteria? A virus? An intestinal worm? An idea. Resilient... highly contagious. Once an idea has taken hold of the brain it's almost impossible to eradicate. An idea that is fully formed – fully understood – that sticks, right in there somewhere."*

I believe he has a point in saying it. There are people who have been possessed by an idea and that idea dictates the direction of their lives and produces an extraordinary passion in achieving it. Individuals who are possessed by an idea are those people who are normally consistent. As Steve Jobs said, *"You have to be burning with an idea, or a problem, or a wrong that you want to right. If you're not passionate enough from the start, you'll never stick it out."*

There could be a lot of sources and motivation that produces passion. Your job is to find that one source where you can acquire that love and commitment to whatever you will do about it. Try to identify it. Do you have a specific talent that you really do well with? Do you have a burden for a specific problem that you want to solve? Or do you have an idea that has the potential to help a lot of people improve their way of life? Try your best to discover the source, and then build your passion around it.

2. Ask Questions

Another way to discover and pursue your passion is to ask yourself a lot of questions. Put yourself in different scenarios and try to think in terms of your possible response to those situations. Also, these theoretical experiments might also reveal the deepest desires of your heart and what are the things that are most important to you. Here are some situational questions that you can ask yourself:

* *If you only have six months to live, what will you do with your remaining days?*
* *If you have inherited a lot of money that you don't need to*

work a day in your life, what are the things that you will
pursue?

- *If you are prohibited in doing all the activities you love to do except one, what will it be?* (necessities are exempted)

Another form of question that you can ask yourself, to discover your passion, is probing questions. This line of questioning aims to bring to light those things that you have loved to do in the past and even those things that you do exceptionally well. Just make sure you are truthful in answering these questions. Don't base your answer on what is ideal; rather respond to it in terms of what happened.

- *What are the things that you are interested and curious about?*
- *What are the things that others find difficult but you can do fairly easy compared to them – and with great results?*
- *What are the things that other people consult you about?*

In addition to the situational and probing questions, you can also ask the three questions that were formulated by John Maxwell in discovering an individual's passion in life. John often asked his audience these three questions to help them find out their true passion. Try answering it and maybe you will find some clues about where your passion is located.

1. *What do you sing about?*

This question aims to shed some light on those things that you are most happy doing. It gives you some clue on what are the things that you look forward to each day. Perhaps you are always excited when meeting with some friends and share your interest with animals. Or maybe you always look forward to your Friday nights where the whole gang will be on a night out in some karaoke club, where you can share your skills in singing.

2. *What do you cry about?*

All of us have this soft spot in our hearts for specific people, things or situations. There are people who care so much for the aged. Others are deeply concerned about the environment. Some individuals have a heart for the abused and helpless.

Here's a simple experiment for you: try to look back at the

videos that you have watched and shared on social media. You can also find some clues on the pages that you liked on Facebook. Try to see a pattern and find out those things that makes you so mad, sad, and hopeful all at the same time.

3. *What do you dream about?*

These are the things that will give you extra fulfillment upon doing. Do you dream about making a significant impact in the lives of the youth in your community? Do you dream of building a foundation to shelter the homeless?

Do you dream of planting trees and building a whole forest?

What do you dream about? And if your dream is bigger than yourself, then congratulations, you have a big clue as to where your passion lies.

Your calling is inevitably connected with your passion. You won't have the heart for something that you despise doing.

Asking yourself these questions might provide the clues that you need to discover your passion. However, it will also be useful that you follow through on the clues that you will find. For instance, if by asking some situational questions, you found out that writing is one of the most important activities in your life that you can never give up, then perhaps that is your passion. Do it more often and assess yourself if you are finding fulfillment in doing it.

Another example would be answering some probing questions; if you realize that people are constantly complimenting your intelligence, then maybe you can be passionate about studying and learning.

3. *Pursue Your Passion*

Passion is not just meant to be known, it is always meant to be pursued. After gaining some clues by asking yourself a lot of questions, it is now the right time to try out some of those things that you find interesting. You won't be able to find out if you are truly passionate for something if you don't see it and do it yourself. During this part of the process, it is also possible to learn that some of the things you are curious about are not really your passion, but some things that you care deeply about are indeed those same things that can give your life a new meaning.

Also, you must understand that pursuing your passion is a gradual process. You don't have to quit your job and leave everything behind just to pursue your passion. The process of pursuing those things that you truly love can begin by setting a tiny portion of your day to try out some new stuff. If you discover that you are interested in learning how to play the guitar and have always been fascinated by people who can play it well, then perhaps you can set aside 30 minutes to an hour a day practicing and learning the skill. The same goes with other skills that you think you can spark the flame of passion in you. There are some people who can discover their passion through this process, so you can try it too for yourself.

It will be helpful if you also associate with people who have a similar interest. Now that we are connected globally with anyone who has access to the internet, you can also join groups, forums and discussion boards that are dedicated to the specific interest, cause, or hobbies that you have. You will find out that it is encouraging to know that there are a lot of people like you who share the same heart when it comes to things. If you are an animal lover, then you will find the company of other animal lovers inspiring and motivating. If you have interest in music, then joining a group of musicians and other music enthusiasts can give you more encouragement in pursuing your passion.

Passion is the main ingredient of Living!

Do you know that you can be dead while at the same time look alive? How is that possible? It's by living your life without a specific calling or passion. Most people are afraid to pursue their passion because of so many other things. They think that when they try to pursue those things that they really love, they will end up broke and disillusioned like so many other people who tried it. For them, the idea of pursuing their passion is too reckless and risky and is only reserved for those who can afford not to work to pay the rent. If you are not that wealthy, but you decide to pursue and stick to your passion, then people will see you as crazy. For them, you are on the path of guaranteed death by starvation. However, looking closely, most of the people that are truly alive and happy are those people who embrace their calling and their passion.

Have you watched the movie entitled *"The Croods?"* It is about a family of cavemen who lived thousands of years ago,. They lived in a harsh and dangerous environment so the head of the family, Grug, established a single rule – *No one is allowed to leave the cave except when they are hunting to eat.* They spent most of their time inside the cave and in fact, to avoid danger, basically, everything was prohibited. However, the main story of the movie revolved around when they were forced to leave their cave because the world was undergoing geological changes.

It was a fun movie to watch as the family tried to do everything to avoid all kinds of peril in their new environment. Yet, Grug always wanted to live in a cave because it was his comfort zone. And in his stubbornness, himself and his daughter, Ip, started to fall out. During one of their quarrels, as Grug forces his family back to the cave because it is the reason that they are alive, Ip uttered the most enigmatic and eye-opening lines of the movie: *"That is not living! That is just not dying! There's a difference."*

A lot of people today are so busy working for a 'living' that they forget to 'live.' In fact, just like what Ip said, they are not living, they are just not dying. When you stop living for a purpose and pursuing your passion, you will begin to die. However, unlike most death, this process will be gradual and you won't be aware of it, until you come to the end of your life and ask yourself, *"Why did I not pursue it?"* My friend, passion is one of the main ingredients to live a fulfilling and satisfying life.

If you still haven't discovered your passion, then I encourage you to start searching for it today. And when you find it, pursue it. Heed the words of Terri Guillemets: *"Chase down your passion like it's the last bus of the night."*

"If you follow your passion, you will realize that your passion is linked to your overall satisfaction in life" – Chindah Chindah

Discussion Questions and Reflections:

This portion of each chapter aims to establish the concepts and principles that you have learned so far. Try to carefully consider each question and answer it with a complete reflection of how it applies to your life. I would also implore you to take notes and even share what you have learned with others to initiate healthy discussion.

1. Passionate people are everywhere. They can be found in your family, your school, or your workplace. Can you identify a person who you consider passionate? What is his or her quality that stands out to you? What are the signs that you can see in him or her that makes you believe that he or she is indeed passionate?

   _____

   _____

   _____

   _____

2. We have discussed three personal accounts of men who have shown great passion in their lives. What specific aspect of their passion stands out to you? What characteristics would you like to imitate of these people? Do you know of other individuals who have exemplified passion in their lives? How can you display that strong passion in the things that you love to do?

   _____

   _____

   _____

   _____

3. Pursuing your passion is not just an option; it is a necessity if you truly want to experience the thrill and excitement of living. Out of the sources of passion that we have outlined in this chapter, what source resonated with you? Answer all the

questions that I laid out in this chapter and see a common theme or clue to what truly is your passion. Lastly, set a plan of how you would start pursuing your passion. Schedule, it and keep yourself accountable with another person.

_____

_____

_____

_____

EPILOGUE

*"If you don't design your own life plan, chances are you'll
fall into someone else's plan. And guess what they have
planned for you? Not much."*

– Jim Rohn

First, I would like to congratulate you on finishing this book. I
sincerely hope you have learned the things you need to begin the
journey of self-improvement, and uncover a lot of nuggets of truth
that can bring you towards your desired destination. However,
despite all the wisdom and information you can find in this book,
everything will be meaningless if there isn't effective follow
through. All the knowledge you have gained and ideas you have
acquired will be wasted if you don't take the opportunity to apply
it to improve your life. And here is where a specific action plan
and strategy is needed.

As you have already realized, things normally don't happen on
their own – especially when it comes to personal growth and self-
improvement. Unlike our bodies which grow automatically
depending on our age, wisdom doesn't come naturally, and applied
wisdom doesn't happen accidentally. As the saying goes,
"Maturity doesn't come with age." Considering this, it is crucial
that you develop and cultivate a detailed action plan to help you in
implementing all the things that you have learned in the last eight
chapters of this book. You must be able to assimilate all the
principles, concepts, and ideas into your everyday and at the same
time, make sure that you won't stop learning new things along the
way.

Here are some tips that you can use in designing your life plan
and integrating the lessons that you have acquired in the pages of
this manuscript:

- ***Think About the Overall Picture*** – to design an effective action plan, you must first need to see the destination of everything that you are doing. Reflect on what would be the final goal of your life. What would be the overarching purpose in everything that you will try to do?

  This activity might require you to seek out your purpose and calling so you can snugly fit the principles in that you have acquired. Here is the idea: *Everything that you do must be connected to this overall goal.*

- ***Create Milestones*** – milestones are significant events or conditions that you want to achieve or accomplish during your pursuit of goals. These can also be landmarks that signify you are coming nearer to your desired destination.

  For instance, if one of your life goals is to set up your own business, then some of the milestones that you might consider would be coming up with a viable business idea, acquiring enough capital, purchasing the required equipment, and finding the right location for your business. Each time that you achieve one of your milestones, it means you are one step closer to your goal.

- ***Formulate strategies to reach your milestones*** – After you have set up the milestones that will bring you closer to your goals, then it's time to formulate the strategies that will help you in achieving them. This is where the principles and concepts that you acquired in this book are useful. The applicable knowledge and teaching must be applied to help you create your strategies.

  Let us take for example the things that you learned in chapter 3 about assessing and utilizing your personal strength assets. Now, since you learned in chapter 3 that you need to play around your strengths if you want to achieve maximum results in your endeavors, then you must consider your skills and expertise when formulating your strategies. Now, if you have a strategy that requires a skill that you don't have, then you can always outsource.

These are just some guidelines that you can use in using the things that you have learned in this book in actual practice. However, depending on your temperament, personalities, and preference, the actual application might vary. If you still don't have a clear grasp of your own uniqueness, then it would be helpful to have some form of assessment to validate these important aspects of yourself. There are a lot of resources online and other books that help you to evaluate yourself in different areas such as temperament, strengths, and aptitude to specific tasks.

Final Challenge

In the closing words of this book, I would like to encourage and challenge you to never stop learning. If this is your first time finishing a book on personal development and self-improvement, then I commend you for doing so and at the same time hope that this will just be the beginning of your quest to continually improve yourself until the day you die. If you have already read a lot of books that deal with the same topics that are presented here, then I hope what you learned here added to the things that you already know and will help you to better pinpoint the areas of your life that still need to be developed.

At the end of this book, I had a simple challenge for you: *Never stop learning.* This shouldn't end now you have finished this one book. I challenge you to seek more wisdom, desire more learning, and obtain more principles, concepts, and ideas.

If by reading this book, you realize there are some areas of your life that still needs a lot of improvement, then get a book, something that is entirely focused on that topic. Maybe it's all about developing your strengths, or maybe it could be about the niche of pursuing your passion, perhaps you need more information about establishing discipline in your life. Whatever it is, don't stop learning and trying to acquire new wisdom.

Also, it would be helpful if you can find a mentor that has already achieved what you want to accomplish. Your mentor doesn't necessarily have to be 10 or eight steps ahead of you. Find someone who is willing to guide you in the process of discovering yourself and growing in your gifts and talents. If it is possible, meet regularly with this mentor as he/she teaches and guides you on what you need to do to experience breakthrough in your life. It would be encouraging also to have an accountability group to discuss your progress and share the things that you are learning with each other. Jim Rohn insightfully asserted that, *"You are the average of the five people you spend the most time with."* So, it would be great to be surrounded by people that have the same passion for growth as you.

However, in the end, everything will rise and fall in your decision. If you decide to find ways how you can apply everything that you learned in the pages of this book, then I guarantee your life will change and so will the lives of the people around you. However if you opt to stay passive and just let the wisdom and ideas that you encountered in this book rot in the recesses of your mind, then I can also guarantee there won't be any significant change or progress when it comes to your growth.

In fact, after several years, you might still find yourself having the same problems, worrying over the same issues, and struggling with the same obstacles because you did not take the initiative to improve yourself now. It doesn't matter if you are on the right track. As Will Rogers said, *"Even if you're on the right track, you'll get run over if you just sit there."*

Lastly, I encourage you to pass on what you have learned. Yes, learning never stops, and learning should never stop with you. Share what you have learned with other people. You don't have to be a teacher to teach others about different principles of life that can be useful for them. I would also encourage you to read the book again, but this time with an expectation and awareness that you will teach what you have learned to other individuals. Think about this; do you believe that teaching others how to pursue their passion can have a significant impact in their lives? Also, if you teach others about the importance of change and that they have the capacity to implement it, don't you think that they can also transform their lives for the better?

My friend, the world is hungry for people who have the guts to take the high road of personal development and self-improvement and who are also willing to take others with them on the journey. I challenge you – be one of those people!

"Knowledge is not power yet, until the knowledge is translated into action and direct application into your daily life" – Chindah Chindah

"The clarity of your vision, will propel you to change for the realization of your vision" – Chindah Chindah

KEY NOTES

Chapter 1

1. *Wealth of the World's Richest People vs GDP of Countries.* (n.d). Retrieved February 15, 2017, from https://knoema.com/infographics/wqezguc/wealth-of-the-world-s-richest-people-vs-gdp-of-countries.

2. Johnetta McSwain, *Rising Above the Scars* (Atlanta: Dream Wright Publications, 2010), 14.

3. Groundhog Day. Dir. Harold Ramis. Columbia Pictures Corporation, 1993. Film.

Chapter 2

1. "Jim Rohn's Biography," JimRohn.com, accessed December 14, 2016, http://www.jimrohn.com/index.php?main_page=page&id=1177.

2. Norman Vincent Peale, *The Power of Positive Thinking,* 13 – 14.

3. Michael Brus, *Self-Loathing Wins Championships.* Retrieved December 14, 2016, from http://www.slate.com/articles/sports/sports_nut/2013/08/tommy_haas_video_what_we_can_learn_about_sports_psychology_by_watching_a.html.

4. Retrieved from http://www.statisticbrain.com/new-years-resolution-statistics/.

Chapter 3

1. "John James Audubon Biography," Audubon.org. Retrieved December 15, 2016, from http://www.audubon.org/content/john-james-audubon.

2. Top 10 Most Intelligent People of the World, Retrieved December 15, 2016, from http://www.wonderslist.com/10-

most-intelligent-people/.

Chapter 4

1. Todd Eliason, *A Life of Leadership and Inspiration.* Retrieved December 17, 2016, from http://www.success.com/article/a-life-of-leadership-and-inspiration.

Chapter 5

1. James Glassman, *An Old Lady's Lesson: Patience Usually Pays,"* Washington Post, December 17, 1995.

2. Natalie Kitroeff, *Have Millennials Made Quitting More Common,"* Bloomberg. Retrieved December 18, 2016, from https://www.bloomberg.com/news/articles/2016-02-12/have-millennials-made-quitting-more-common.

3. John C. Maxwell, *The 15 Invaluable Laws of Growth,* pp. 144.

4. Proverbs 27:17 NIV.

Chapter 6

1. Genesis 37 – 50 NIV.

2. Stephen Covey, *The 7 Habits of Highly Effective People,* pp.

3. Portia Nelson, *There's a Hole in My Sidewalk: The Romance of Self-Discovery,* 1973.

Chapter 7

1. Natalie Angier, *Why Men Don't Last: Self-Destruction as a Way of Life,* New York Times. Retrieved January 10, 2016, from http://www.nytimes.com/1999/02/17/health/why-men-don-t-last-self-destruction-as-a-way-of-life.html.

Chapter 8

1. Cavedigger Documentary. Dir. Jeffrey Karoff. KAROFFilms, 2015. Documentary.

2. La La Land. Dir. Damien Chazelle. Summit Entertainment, 2016. Film.

3. "The Life of Churchill", WinstonChurchill.org, retrieved January 15, 2016 from http://www.winstonchurchill.org/the-life-of-churchill/life.

4. "Martin Luther King, Jr. and the Global Freedom Struggle", retrieved January 15, 2016 from http://kingencyclopedia.stanford.edu/encyclopedia/enc yclopedia/enc_martin_luther_k ing_jr_biography/.

5. "Gandhi's Life in 5,000 Words," MKGandhi.org, retrieved January 15, 2016 from http://www.mkgandhi.org/bio5000/bio5index.htm.

OTHER BOOKS BY CHINDAH CHINDAH

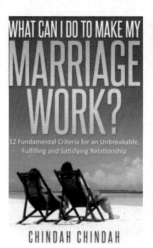 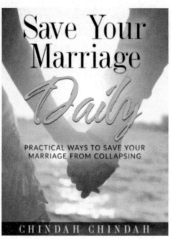

These books will be available in the following formats: Hardcopy, softcopy, kindle, Ebook and audio in various popular book platforms online and retailers. You can find more information on the websites below for release dates.

www.chindahchindah.com
www.4xlpublishing.com

Note

Note

Note

Note

Note

Note

Note

Note

Note

Note

Note

Note